THE TROUBLE WITH STRATEGY...

THE TROUBLE WITH STRATEGY...

Kim Warren

Published by   Strategy Dynamics Limited,
                    Two Farthings,
                    Aylesbury Rd,
                    Princes Risborough
                    HP27 0JS, England.
                    T +44 (0) 1844 275518.
                    www.strategydynamics.com

Copyright © 2012   Kim Warren

All brand names, company names and product names used in this book are trade names, service marks, trademarks or registered trademarks of their respective owners.

This publication is intended to provide accurate and authoritative information in regard to the subject matter covered. Its contents do not represent recommendations for any specific circumstance, for which the advice of a competent professional should be sought.

Kim Warren has asserted his right under the Copyright, Designs and Patents Act 1988, to be identified as the author of this work.

The cartoons were created by "Higgins" of HigginsCartoons.com.

British Library Cataloguing in Publication Data.
A catalogue record for this book is available from the British Library.

To Christina - my dear wife and much-loved partner
in this and other efforts over so many years.

Acknowledgements.

My greatest appreciation goes to Jeremy Kourdi - writer and executive coach. Jeremy pointed me to many of the issues and examples in the book, as well as contributing many of the words.

I owe a big debt of thanks to the many, many people who have inspired this book and provided ideas, examples and guidance – business colleagues, academics who share a deep frustration with the strategy field, students and executive with stories of the problems they face. All have been kind and generous with their time,and I should apologise to them for taking so long to decide the time is right for the book to appear.

Unfortunately, since I do not want them to be attacked for the views I have wrapped around their contributions, I think it wise not to name them, but you know who you are!

Contents

THE EMPEROR'S NEW CLOTHES

Adapted from the tale by Hans Christian Andersen...

An emperor was so excessively fond of new clothes that he spent all his money in dress. He had a different suit for each hour of the day; and it was always said of him, "The Emperor is sitting in his wardrobe."

One day, two rogues, calling themselves weavers, made their appearance. They gave out word that they knew how to weave cloth of the most beautiful colours and elaborate patterns. Clothes made from this material would have the wonderful property of remaining invisible to everyone who was unfit for the office he held, or who was extraordinarily simple in character.

"These must, indeed, be splendid clothes!" thought the Emperor. "Had I such a suit, I might at once find out which men in my realms are unfit for their office, and be able to distinguish the wise from the foolish!"

So the two weavers set up looms and pretended to work very busily, though in reality they did nothing at all. They asked for the most delicate silk and the purest gold thread but put these into their own bags, then continued their pretended work.

"I should like to know how the weavers are getting on with my cloth," said the Emperor to himself after some little time had elapsed. "I will send my faithful old minister to the weavers," said the Emperor at last after some deliberation. "He will be best able to see how the cloth looks, for he is a man of sense, and no one can be more suitable for his office than he is."

So the faithful old minister went into the hall, where the knaves were working at their empty looms. "What can be the meaning of this?" thought the old man, opening his eyes very wide. "I cannot discover the least bit of thread on the looms." The impostors asked him whether the design pleased him, and whether the colours were not very beautiful. The poor old minister looked and looked but could not discover anything on the looms, for there was nothing to be seen. "Is it possible that I am a simpleton? Can it be that I am unfit for my office? No, that must not be said either. I will never confess that I could not see the stuff."

"Oh, it is excellent!" replied the old minister, looking at the loom through his spectacles. "This pattern, and the colours, yes, I will tell the Emperor without delay, how very beautiful I think them."

"We shall be much obliged to you," said the impostors, who proceeded to name the different colours and describe the pattern of the pretended material. However, they continued to put all the material they were given into their bags and continued to work with as much apparent diligence at their empty looms.

The Emperor now sent another officer of his court to see how the men were getting on. "Does not the stuff appear as beautiful to you as it did to my lord, the minister?" asked the impostors of the Emperor's second ambassador. "I certainly am not stupid!" thought the messenger. "It must be that I am not fit for my good, profitable office; however, no one shall know anything about it." And accordingly he praised the cloth he could not see. The whole city was now talking of the splendid material which the Emperor had ordered to be woven.

And now the Emperor himself wished to see the costly cloth, so he went to the crafty impostors. "Is not the work absolutely magnificent?" asked the two officers of the crown, already mentioned. "If your Majesty will only be pleased to look at it! What a splendid design! What glorious colours!"

"How is this?" said the Emperor to himself. "I can see nothing! Am I a simpleton, or am I unfit to be an Emperor? That would be the worst thing that could happen!"

"Oh! The cloth is charming," said he, aloud. All his retinue now strained their eyes, but they could see no more than the others. Nevertheless, they all exclaimed, "Oh, how beautiful!" and advised his majesty to have some new clothes made from this splendid material for the approaching procession.

The rogues sat up the whole of the night before the procession, with lights burning, so everyone might see how anxious they were to finish the Emperor's new suit. They pretended to roll out the cloth, cut the air with their scissors, and sewed with needles without any thread in them. "See!" they cried at last. "The Emperor's new clothes are ready!"

And now the Emperor, with all the grandees of his court, came to the weavers, and the rogues raised their arms, as if in the act of holding something up, saying, "Here are your Majesty's trousers! Here is the scarf! Here is the cloak! The whole suit is as light as a cobweb; one might fancy one has nothing on at all when dressed in it. That, however, is the great virtue of this delicate cloth."

"Yes, indeed!" said all the courtiers, although not one of them could see anything of this exquisite clothing. "If your Imperial Majesty will be graciously pleased to take off your clothes, we will fit on the new suit in front of the looking glass."

The Emperor was undressed, and the rogues pretended to array him in his new suit; the Emperor turning round, from side to side, before the looking glass. "How splendid his Majesty looks in his new clothes, and how well they fit!" everyone cried out. "What a design! What colours! These are indeed royal robes!"

"I am quite ready," answered the Emperor. "Do my new clothes fit well?" he asked, turning himself round again before the looking glass, so he might appear to be examining his handsome suit. The lords of the bedchamber, who were to carry his Majesty's train felt about on the ground, as if they were lifting up the ends of the cloak and pretended to be carrying something; for they would by no means betray that they were unfit for their office.

So now the Emperor walked under his high canopy in the midst of the procession, through the streets of his capital. And all the people standing by, and those at the windows, cried out, "Oh! How beautiful are our Emperor's new clothes! What a magnificent train there is to the cloak, and how gracefully the scarf hangs!" In short, no one would admit that he could not see these much admired clothes, because in doing so, he would have declared himself either a simpleton or unfit for his office. Certainly, none of the Emperor's various suits had ever made so great an impression as these invisible ones.

"But the Emperor has nothing on at all!" said a little child.

"Listen to the voice of innocence!" exclaimed the child's father, and what the child had said was whispered from one to another.

"But he has nothing on at all!" at last cried out all the people. The Emperor was vexed, for he knew that the people were right, but he thought the procession must go on! And the lords of the bedchamber took greater pains than ever to appear to be holding up a train, although, in reality, there was no train to hold.

The End

So is "strategy", too, an invisible cloak, hiding lack of competence?

January 2008: Starbucks fires its CEO, before reporting later in the year a substantial drop in profits that continued into 2009.

October 2008: Fred Goodwin resigns as CEO of Royal Bank of Scotland, shortly before the bank reported the largest financial loss ever recorded by a UK corporation, and less than one year after reporting record profits.

September 2009: eBay sells majority ownership of Skype, writing off US$1.39 billion just four years after buying the company for US$3.1 billion.

September 2011: Yahoo! fires its CEO after a drop in revenue and profits, allegedly due to a partnership with Microsoft.

September 2011: Hewlett-Packard fires its CEO, just a year after joining the company and laying out a new strategy.

November 2011: CEO of Cable & Wireless departs after growth and morale had fallen to an all-time low because of changes of strategy.

INTRODUCTION

The economic turmoil of 2008–09 added to an already growing crisis of public trust in corporations and their leaders, not only in banking, but in manufacturing, retail, transportation. In sector after sector, corporations woke up to the reality that gravity had not been abolished and that the unending growth forecasts upon which their foolish expansion plans relied had never been realistic. Capacity increases were canned, supplier orders pulled, and employees laid off, actions that added to the crisis that engulfed them all, and from which they were still struggling to drag themselves three years later.

Some, who focus only on a handful of egregious examples, claim that these difficulties reflect a widespread lack of ethics and bad governance. But executives as a breed are not by and large unprincipled villains, pocketing loads of cash whilst leaving investors with crumbs. Most are able, committed, and responsible people trying to do their best. If they could have done better, they would have.

The real question then is not about ethics or governance, but about whether business leaders actually know how to deliver long-term performance. The evidence suggests that many do not[1]—which is pretty disappointing, because that is exactly what *strategic* management is supposed to deliver.

But why should *you* care about something so rarefied and distant from your everyday concerns as "strategy"? Because it's not distant—it has a very real impact on you, your family, and on society. As serious as the recession was, it is merely a symptom of a much bigger problem: that long-run business performance is generally not very good!

You should care if you are an employee. The least you might expect at work, apart from not being injured, is that your organisation will be competently steered from year to year so that you can enjoy a stable working life. Bad strategic management has destroyed the livelihoods of ordinary people in airlines (Swissair and Japan Airlines), telecoms (GEC/Marconi, Global Crossing, and Iridium), financial services (Washington Mutual and Northern Rock), auto manufacture (General Motors and the British Motor Industry).[2] The human cost can be on a truly industrial scale, as in the decades-long demise of US and UK car companies, the high-tech failures of the 2000–01 dot-com bust, and the 2008–09 banking collapse.

You should care if you have a pension or insurance. The investment firms who look after your money put much of it into company stocks. They expect it to grow so they can pay out what you hoped for when you paid in your premiums. If the companies they invest in mess up, it costs *you!* As of today, there is no need for senior executives to prove any competence at strategic management. But neither is there any requirement for those who manage your money to show they understand anything about the link between how firms are managed and their financial performance.[3] And it shows: investment firms persistently over-estimate companies' profit growth by a huge margin, putting pressure on management to deliver short-term results by taking actions that destroy *future* performance.[4]

You should care if you are a consumer. Bad strategic management means you get offered products and services that don't suit your needs by organisations that cannot provide or support them properly. Although we all love the low-priced, reliable travel offered by the Southwest Airlines, Ryanairs, and easyJets of the airline industry, it's not been much fun being served by most of the 40-odd copycats who tried to do the same in Europe during the last decade but have now failed. And how many consumers got burned by sub-prime mortgages? Plausible salespeople pushed people into borrowing money on which they could never repay either the interest or capital, leaving them either homeless or with debts that would cripple them for decades. And that is just those who felt the most direct harm; millions more saw vast sums wiped from their personal wealth as property values crashed.

You should care if you are a manager—at any level. For every CEO, CFO, and COO, hundreds of senior, middle, and junior managers work hard to help their organisations do well. Surveys regularly find that these folk mostly don't understand or respect their companies' strategies.[5]. They just get on with the job, trying to cope as best they can when management, in pursuit of strategy innovation or some other fad, change everything around instead of focusing on continuous, strong development. And it's these regular Joes and Janes who pay the price of trying to do the impossible and have to sort out the mess afterwards, a price that can include the destruction of their careers and their families' well-being.

… and everyone else should care. Strategy failures mess up the entire economy, destroying jobs and wealth on a vast scale. Aside from wars and other big shocks, most recessions start in the corporate sector (see Figure 1).[6] Corporate reversals are not typically triggered by cutbacks made by consumers or government, but by the too-late dawning of reality on over-extended companies. Confidence too easily turns to recklessness after a few years of good business opportunities and the rah-rah encouragement from analysts, journalists, and others who do not actually share management's responsibility for sound long-term strategy. The recessions of 2001–02 and 2008–09 threw millions out of work, and devastated tax revenues that would otherwise have funded public services and supported those who cannot be economically active. There is no divine authority imposing economic booms and busts on unfortunate business leaders— they are caused by executives themselves making ill-advised business decisions, encouraged by analysts with no understanding of strategy and performance.

Figure 1: How the corporate sector led the US into the 2008-09 recession

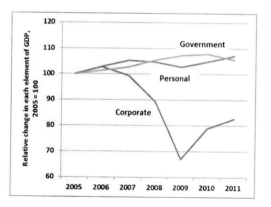

When leaders mess up strategy, they mess up YOUR life!

Headline-making disasters are bad enough, but these are merely the tip of a big, dark iceberg. What you never hear of are the majority of organisations who plod forward from year to year, failing frustratingly to make the progress that they could and should make, or making non-fatal errors that nevertheless destroy value, demoralise staff, and abuse customers. Starbucks has long been feted for its great products, clever people-management policies, and staggering growth. Yet between 2003 and 2007, it took $400 million[7] of extra profit from customers by raising prices and margins, while at the same time wasting a similar sum by opening 500 stores it later had to close when customers took a poor view of Starbucks' value for money and stayed away.

To be clear here: people are *not* generally bad at management. Most are skilled at the functional job they do. Marketing executives know how to win customers; heads of production know how to get good products out reliably and efficiently; senior accounting folk know how to look after a company's finances. These same people may be just great at getting things done, leading others, and managing teams. Rather, we will see that—no matter how proficient managers are at these other tasks—their organisations stumble or fail because of poor *strategic* management.

This failure is not their fault. After the decades of research, thousands of articles and books published, and millions of hours invested in understanding strategy, we should expect that executives are better informed and educated. The fact that they aren't is not evidence that they are unintelligent or incompetent, but that they do not have the tools and skills to do better.

You should be worried about this if you are studying management, whether on executive courses or in degree courses. If you are not taught anything useful, then you will have wasted time and money, and emerge into management ill-equipped to do any aspect of your job that involves strategy. And don't imagine that strategic management is only for those at the top. In today's complex and fast-moving world we can no longer rely on the command-and-control systems of the past: *you* will be making decisions of strategic importance, too, so you had better know how.

4

You should be worried about all this if you teach strategy. As we will show, few executives apply what business schools teach them about strategy, and virtually none use any of the research you so painstakingly—and expensively—generate. And the best management consulting firms think so little of business school strategy teaching that in just a few weeks they give any bright recruit—whatever their previous professional background—the essential skills they think are needed, and which few business graduates have gained over a one- to two-year program.

The business school community—particularly those academics focusing on strategy—are not entirely complacent about this. There has been a long-running and growing debate, dating back at least to the mid-1990s, about the increasing irrelevance of business school teaching and strategy research.[8] So the strategy professors are certainly looking for explanations for the problems we have started to describe in this Introduction. We should all hope they find those answers and figure a way out.

Lastly, a little about the me...

I started on strategy in the oil and petrochemicals industry, before heading the strategy design to transform Whitbread PLC from a threatened brewing company into the restaurant and hotel power-house it has since become. I then spent several years at London Business School, teaching conventional approaches to strategy on MBA and Executive programs, before realising they offered little value. I have since developed a rigorous, practical approach to developing and managing strategy - fully aligned with the needs of management and investors to build value - known as Strategy Dynamics. My time is now spent writing and developing courses on the approach, and advising corporate clients on its use. I have an MBA and PhD from LBS and am author of the textbook Strategic Management Dynamics (Wiley) and the executive e-book Strategy Dynamics Essentials.

Notes

1. A 10-year study by consultants Bain & Company found that only 12% of 2000 quoted companies delivered sustained value creation, defined as growing revenue and profits by at least 5.5% per year, and returning the cost of capital to shareholders. See Chris Zook and James Allen, 2010, Profit from the Core: A Return to Growth in Turbulent Times, Boston: Bain & Company, Inc. See also Chris Zook, 2007, Unstoppable: Finding Hidden Assets to Renew the Core and Fuel Profitable Growth, Boston: Bain & Company, Inc..

2. Links to relavent stories on these companies can be found on the "Trouble with Strategy" website - www.troublewithstrategy.com

3. The Chartered Financial Analysts Institute (CFAI) qualifies people to practise in the investment industry. It has over 100,000 charter holders operating in 130 countries worldwide. Yet curiously, there is nothing in its training programs to explain how a company's strategic management affects its financial performance. See the CFAI's Body of Knowledge. Retrieved 28-3-2012.

4. Marc Goedhart, Rishi Raj, and Abhishek Saxena, 2010, "Equity Analysts: Still Too Bullish", McKinsey Quarterly, April. Retrieved 28-3-2012.

5. See, for example, Robert Kaplan and David Norton, 2005, "The Office of Strategy Management", Harvard Business Review, 83(10), October, pp. 72–81.

6. Paul Ormerod, 2011, "The Key Empirical Features of Economic Recessions under Capitalism", Keynote presentation at the International Scientific Symposium Devoted to the 110th Anniversary of Simon Kuznets, Kiev.

7. Unless otherwise stated, all financial amounts are given in US dollars.

8. Paula Jarzabkowski and Richard Whittington, 2008, Directions for a Trouble Discipline, Journal of Management Inquiry, 17(4), pp.266-268.

9. Constantinos C. Markides, 2000, All the Right Moves: A Guide to Crafting Breakthrough Strategy. Boston: Harvard Business School Press, pp. 27–112.

CHAPTER ONE

THE GOOD, THE BAD, AND THE UGLY

"But he has nothing at all on!" at last cried out all the people. The emperor was vexed, for he knew that the people were right; but he thought the procession must go on!

From The Emperor's New Clothes by Hans Christian Andersen.

Before we look at a few cases of good and poor strategy, it will help to have some idea of what "strategy" actually is. Many complicated and abstract answers to this question can be found, but a simple definition is enough for now:

An organisation's strategy is how it tries to reach its objectives.

This implies that "strategic management" includes the following:

1. **Choosing objectives for the organisation**. Objectives may be financial, such as growth in cash flow, or non-financial, such as reaching some number of customers by some point in time. Objectives can be ambitious, but do not have to be, and they may need to be adjusted as conditions change.

2. **Selecting what the organisation will do, compared with other organisations**. In business cases, this means deciding which customers to serve, with which products or services, and how this will be done. Non-business organisations, from schools to voluntary groups to churches, also choose which services to offer, to which, beneficiaries, and how.

3. **Steering progress over time.** Having decided on a position that offers the potential for success, management must continually build the necessary resources and capabilities, and develop effective policies to steer its strategy and performance as circumstances change. This is more than simply the sum of good decision-making in each function of the business. Decisions on product development, marketing, staff development, pricing, and so on must work well together and adapt so they continue to do so as circumstances change.

Good performance over long periods of time suggests that executives do all of these tasks well. Failure to make that progress, serious setbacks, or total collapse imply that one or more of them has been done badly.

The good

Let's start on a positive note by recognising that some outstanding strategic management **does** happen. There are many fine examples of organisations developing good strategies, implementing them well for many years, and when necessary, making big moves that deliver still further results, all without taking too much risk.

Just a word of warning, though. There is a common tendency in strategy writing to look for success stories and then hold those cases up as infallible role models for all to follow. (Where, we wonder, did all the eulogies about Enron, WorldCom, and Royal Bank of Scotland disappear to after their spectacular demises? Where are the analysts who recommended Lehman Brothers a "buy" almost to the day it became the largest banking bankruptcy in the meltdown of 2008–09?)[1]. We will not make the same mistake here. Indeed, some examples will appear on both sides of the balance sheet: doing strategy outstandingly well in some circumstances, and making fundamental errors at other times.

Success may turn to failure for a host of reasons. New management may alter the processes and procedures that drove earlier achievements. Previous sources of success may become obsolete or overtaken by competitors. And new challenges may require resources or capabilities we do not possess and cannot easily acquire. We should not be surprised, then, when yesterday's heroes stumble.

8

The better news is that the opposite is also true: organisations managing strategy poorly *can* learn to do better. Jim Collins' study of companies that broke through from under-performance to sustained success offers several examples of companies that achieved exactly that turnaround, on a grand scale, and continued their recovery for many more years, companies such as Nucor in steel, Kimberly-Clark in hygiene products, and Pitney-Bowes in mailing equipment[2].

We see different indicators of success in different circumstances. For companies exploiting new opportunities, the clearest evidence may show up in the speed with which they capture the potential they have identified. Skype, the voice-over-Internet protocol (VOIP) phone service, started in 2003, had 560 million user accounts by the end of 2009, and served over 110 billion call minutes in that year — 13 percent of global telephony traffic[3]. Facebook, launched in 2004, had by 2010 over 500 million active users, half of whom used the service on any day.

Businesses offering goods or services based on physical assets may not be able to easily match the stellar achievements of these e-world superstars, but they can still grow impressively. Zipcar, the world's largest car-sharing business, launched in 2000, and by the time of its 2010 IPO had 400,000 members in 13 major metropolitan areas, and was booking 2.6 million reservations per year to generate over $130 million in revenue. It had also just acquired the UK business Streetcar.

Our modern age may seem to run at a frenetic pace, especially in the online world, where no physical products have to be made, transported, or stored. But strong growth is not a new phenomenon. The Blockbuster video-rental business, whose store-based business was brought low by home-delivery and online rivals Netflix and Amazon, originally grew to dominate its sector in the US in just eight years, from 1987 to 1995, before reaching out to capture the same opportunity in other countries. Going back still further, the UK's Lever brothers, who founded the modern soap industry in 1885, had by 1900 created and captured an entire new consumer market and started subsidiaries in North America, Australia, and various European countries.

Before moving on to some precautions, note that good strategy is not all about the market-facing end of the business; it also needs solid choices and effective implementation in the engine room that develops, produces, and supplies a company's products or services. We could review a lot of great practices on everything from product development to manufacturing to IT strategy, but let's take a staffing example. It is now almost obligatory in corporate reporting to include the boilerplate statement "People are our most important asset". But few organisations do quite so much to build and sustain this asset as Indian outsource supplier of information systems, Infosys[4]. The company recognises the intense war for young IT talent in which they are engaged, plus the too-slow output of potential employees to hire from schools. So Infosys reaches way back, not just into university classrooms, but into the school system itself, training teachers and supporting classes to generate the flow of talent that it will need in future, rather than fighting it out day to day with competitors.

Good strategy, then, is not just about a few brilliant choices at particular points in time, but is continually developed and reinforced to carry a company from being a bright, first-to-market entity through the challenges of maturity, dealing with competition and staying relevant throughout its life.

All that glitters may not be gold

Sooner or later, though, sheer activity must translate into financial returns, both to fund further growth and for investors to be interested. In some cases, the business model is so powerful and the need for investment in physical assets and marketing so limited that profitability is almost immediate. Google, for example, has been strongly profitable throughout its short but spectacular life. Perhaps more impressive still are those cases that do demand heavy investment but still manage to deliver strong returns almost from the start. America's Southwest Airlines and Europe's Ryanair both delivered high profitability through most of their fastest years of growth, even though the industry is a notoriously tough one in which to make money. And both have remained relatively successful in financial terms in the face of huge challenges in more recent years.

It is sometimes less clear that other high-profile growth cases will ever make worthwhile profits. Skype mostly lost money until 2008, when it made just $23 million on $551 million of revenue[5]. —this in a global telephony market worth over $1 trillion and making $300 billion in profits. Zipcar was still losing money at the time of its IPO and said it did not know if losses would continue. As it turned out, the company was able to turn in profits for 2011. In purely financial terms, then, some successes that grab the headlines are either trivial in scale or actually unsuccessful. But patience may pay off. Amazon.com, for example, delivered only losses for its first four years, before the huge investment in facilities and systems fulfilled their purposes and the company started to make profits.

Steady as she goes

In contrast to these frisky new enterprises, large companies in mature industries are doing well if they sustain strong cash flows, even if growth is only limited. They achieve this by relentless pursuit of strategies that work, with incremental adjustments, rather than gee-whiz big initiatives.

The auto industry has been mature for decades, in the sense that most markets in the world offer only slow growth and the major competitors have largely remained unchanged. In the ten years to 2008, the worldwide leader Toyota grew its vehicle sales by just 7 percent per year, and its operating profit by just over 10 percent per year. This may not seem spectacular, but look where it has taken the company. Toyota is now the dominant force in the industry and has achieved this position with no grand acquisitions, no strategic transformations, and no "blue ocean"[6] strategy—just unremitting, year-on-year progress.

Banking is also a mature industry. Remember the worldwide banking crisis that nearly wiped out banks across the developed economies? Not in Canada[7], it didn't. Canadian banks not only survived the meltdown, but mostly carried on generating quite decent returns while their foolish brethren in the US and Europe reported huge losses and write-downs.

The mature retail grocery market boasts powerful companies, such as Walmart and Tesco, that drive relentlessly forward, taking business from competitors and delivering rock-solid cash flows. Each of these companies spotted many years ago the opportunity to take a dominant place in their industry with a subtle but important proposition—mid-sized towns for Walmart and out-of-town superstores for Tesco, then pressed forward powerfully with that advantage before, more recently, adding adjustments to the proposition to extend their reach and dominance still further.

Old-economy industrial sectors, too, feature solid performers who just keep delivering. Indian steel giant Tata, now a $30-billion turnover company, has grown nearly five-fold in the last 15 years, whilst at the same time

11

increasing profitability to the point where it regularly delivers over 20-percent profit margins and very healthy returns on capital employed. In this case, acquisitions did play a role, with Tata taking over company after company and imposing effective and efficient management.

Successful though these and other leading companies are, commentators have a curious habit of comparing them with emergent super stars to imply that they are somehow under-achieving. "Who would have thought," says Jim Collins in Good to Great, "that Fannie Mae would beat companies like GE and Coca-Cola? Or that [pharmacy chain] Walgreens could beat Intel?" But of course they would! The supposedly under-performing giants already delivered the returns from dominating their sectors, and do brilliantly to stay on top.

When the road runs out

There is one group of heroes that never gets a mention: people who successfully manage an organisation's decline. Some industries simply die, along with the companies they consist of. Changing technology is often to blame, as when transistors replaced vacuum tubes in electronics applications in the 1960s, or when digital cameras replaced photographic film. Understanding how to squeeze value out of the final years of a business's life is especially important now, in an era when online services are strangling the life out of many face-to-face business models.

Assuming you have been alert enough to see the threat early on, the apparently obvious response to the imminent end of your world is to innovate your way into doing something new. But starting a new business does not make the challenge of the old one disappear. Someone *still* had to manage Kodak's declining photo-film business, even if others had succeeded in building a strong alternative. Ultimately Kodak failed in both tasks. But it was Kodak's main rival, Fuji, who showed just how to manage strategy in a declining industry, at least for a useful number of years. Between 1990 and 2002, driven by clever development of more popular products at better prices, Fujifilm's worldwide share grew from 15 percent to nearly 40 percent, while Kodak's share fell from 60 percent to less than 35 percent[8]. Sure, Fuji was growing share in a shrinking market, so eventually sales collapsed, but they certainly squeezed value out of that decline.

Benefits for all

Whether in cases of growth, maturity, or decline, the benefits of good strategic management are not limited to the financial returns enjoyed by investors. Other stakeholders also do well from the professionalism of these companies.

Customers enjoy good products, services, and support. Staff do well, too. These companies provide stable employment and reasonable incomes, and their growth enables that stability to be shared by increasing numbers of people. Apart from end-of-life cases, suppliers see increasing or sustained demand for *their* products and services, enabling them to plan their own development.

If such professionalism were more widespread, society would benefit, too, from strong streams of taxation and not having to pick up the tab when people are thrown out of work. Even the environment can benefit, since solid companies avoid the waste of resources arising from ill-conceived development.

But some less obvious advantages can get overlooked. Sound strategy eliminates the time and effort that companies often devote to arguing about it. Relationships amongst the executive team can be more positive and rewarding when they are not in constant dispute and not wasting effort on doing the wrong things. Life is easier for everyone. Put simply, it's just plain *nicer* to be part of an organisation that is confidently going about its business!

So what can we learn?

Now you might think that if you want to know how to manage strategy, it would be useful to look at firms who have done well and look for common features of how they do it. There is a long history of such studies, and their results have appeared in various forms, from the frameworks taught in business schools to the advisory procedures of the strategy consulting firms, to popular business books.

Unfortunately, whilst these studies and publications include some excellent research and insight, none seem to answer the key question of *strategy*: how exactly to arrive at a continuous series of choices and decisions, across all parts of the business, under ever-changing conditions, that reinforce each other to grow and sustain strong cash flows. Some look for just a single answer: success is all about choosing the right competitive position, or taking first or second spot in your industry, or being highly innovative, and so on.

Others look for "recipes" of decisions that seem to work. Tom Peters and Robert Waterman's *In Search of Excellence*, for example, reported on a study by consultants McKinsey & Company that apparently found that successful companies exhibited strong links among their strategy, structure, and culture[9]. It did not, however, spell out the actual *strategies* of those companies, nor the steps they took to succeed.

Still others focus intently on how the business was managed but say nothing about what was actually done or why. Jim Collins' *Good to Great* offers useful insights into the process by which management was able to turn companies around, but like *In Search of Excellence*, says nothing about the strategic choices and decisions that actually delivered that success. So it is difficult to extract any transferable strategy-making skills from the cases that are offered.

The bad

Poor, but not disastrous, strategic management comes in many forms. The easiest to spot examples are one-off errors that clearly have negative outcomes, for example, diversifications that should never have been undertaken, misguided entry into new markets, or acquisitions that were never going to deliver any benefits.

When the low-fare airline industry was just ramping up in Europe, established airlines naturally worried that they might lose passengers and revenues. British Airways and KLM both responded by starting their own in-house, low-fare operations. But both companies had to compromise their low-fare strategy with their core business; neither company had the capability to match the leading innovators, Ryanair and easyJet; and neither managed to achieve worthwhile success. Both ended up selling off their mistaken new ventures.

Ill-judged entry into new-country markets seems to be an error to which retailers are especially prone. Now there's nothing wrong with believing that foreign ventures might work; plenty of retailers have been successful in such endeavours. The error lies in persisting with the effort when there is no evidence of its working. UK quality-clothing retailer Marks & Spencer beat a retreat[12] and sold off its US menswear business, Brooks Brothers, at a knock-down price *thirteen years* after it had acquired the company. Many retailers successfully replicate their operations in new country markets, albeit with adjustments to reflect local differences, but Marks seems never even to have *tried* to copy in the US the business model that had been so successful in the UK.

Not everyone takes quite so long to read the writing on the wall. In 2002, Egg Banking, an Internet-only banking service launched by insurer Prudential PLC, decided to build on its UK success by offering the benefits of its credit card to French consumers. The proposition never took off, but it was not until 2004 that the company finally recognised that the French were far less keen on credit cards than the British, favouring store cards instead, and withdrew.

Away from international retailing, some are much quicker to undo mistakes. Netflix, who up until July 2011 provided both DVDs and Internet-streamed video content as a combined subscription, seriously annoyed customers by starting to charge for each service separately. It then compounded the error by announcing that the two services would split completely, thus restricting customers' choice or forcing them to pay twice. Wisely, the company responded to the storm of anger quickly and reversed course by October of the same year[11]. But what kind of strategic analysis led Netflix to think such a strategy was a good idea in the first place?

Buy, buy, buy!

Studies over many decades have found that most acquisitions destroy value for the acquiring firm, but this does not seem to stem the steady stream of badly mistaken acquisitions. Perhaps it is the ego-boost CEOs get from doing big deals, or the relentless pressure from investment banks wanting the fees for facilitating those deals, but for some reason companies seem unable to resist the temptation. The 1998 acquisition of US automaker Chrysler by the normally cool-headed Germans at Daimler-Benz was lauded as a marriage made in heaven. Chrysler would benefit from the brilliant engineering at Mercedes, while the Germans would learn how to make cars with more financial efficiency. Unfortunately, Chrysler was bought as the automotive market peaked, there was no effective strategy for enacting the cross-fertilisation that was supposed to be so beneficial, and the management cultures were about as similar as chalk and cheese. After nearly a decade of trying unsuccessfully to make something of its purchase, Daimler-Benz finally gave up and actually *paid* a purchaser, the private equity firm Cerberus, to take the liability off its hands.

Businesses in the new information economy can also be tempted into the acquisition error. Up until 2005, eBay had been very successful, becoming by far the largest Internet-trading service. Their positioning—who they served, with what, and how—was essentially simple, and it was implemented and driven forward mostly very well. Their early growth had, in real terms, exceeded what Dell and Microsoft had achieved in their early years, and was on a par with Google.

Then in 2005, eBay bought Skype for $2.6 billion, boasting to investors of its "expanding vision". The move would, it claimed, accelerate its own growth, offer new ways to make money from e-commerce, remove a key friction in its business model (presumably some difficulty for buyers and sellers in communicating with each other), and open up unspecified new lines of business. Yet just one year later, eBay had to write off $0.9 billion in goodwill, due to reduced performance expectations, and absorb hundreds of millions in other costs. They also parted with Skype's founder. eBay said they felt Skype could have done a better job of finding other areas for growth and monetization, which is curious, since this was supposed to be one of the *benefits* of the link-up in the first place. More curious still was the 2007 announcement by eBay that, far from integrating the businesses, "Skype had become a much stronger, more focused business." As is so often the case, it was hoped that new leadership would offer the solution to a senseless strategy, but by 2009 it was clear the marriage had not worked, and Skype went its own way.

Pushing too far

Also easy to spot are cases where persistent pursuit of wrong policy over long periods of time builds up trouble that eventually sparks a reversal and correction. How exactly did Starbucks slip up in the period leading up to its profit fall in 2008–09? Between 2002 and 2007, the company added over 9000 new stores, 7000 of which were in the US. Now there is a simple, well-known mechanism in retailing that the more stores you add in an area, the less business the next one you open will

16

likely win, because each new unit has fewer remaining consumers to serve. The new store can appear more successful than it really is by taking business from existing stores, but any skilled retailer should be able to spot this illusion. Starbucks, though, built a store portfolio with a long "tail" of 500 marginal units that, when trading conditions worsened, turned negative and had to be sold. The cost of this mistake? At least $400 million.

Interestingly, $400 million is just about the same amount as that of the additional profit that the company made during the same period by increasing its operating margin from 9.6 percent to over 11 percent. Great achievement, you might think, except that this period also saw the company's premium positioning in the market challenged by lower-priced rivals like McDonald's and rising complaints about the high price of Starbucks' products. And this seemingly modest increase in profitability is worse than it seems. If, over the same period, the company were opening large numbers of increasingly marginal stores, the *sustainable* profitability would have fallen, so a 9.6-percent operating margin on a smaller number of high-quality stores would imply a reasonable expectation of maybe 7 percent, 5 percent, or even less for a much larger estate of weaker stores.

Should Starbucks have seen this coming? Well, in 2001 McDonald's found itself having made *exactly* the same mistakes, and actually stated it publicly in its 2002 Annual Report. Its former CEO was recalled to fix the problem (a step also taken by Starbucks in 2008). In a letter to shareholders, he stated that the business was "…in transition from a company that emphasizes 'adding restaurants to customers' to one that emphasizes 'adding customers to restaurants'. He also targeted a lower rate of profit growth than before, effectively telling investors and analysts to be sensible in their expectations for a mature company. The result? An increased stock price and strongly rising profits.

... and not pushing enough

The tougher cases to spot, although they are extremely common, concern persistent failure to manage strategy well *enough*. Not only is there no clear event in such cases to which subsequent performance can be traced, but that performance may not even have been so bad: the company continues adequately, maybe growing somewhat, and remaining profitable. The failure is not that things have gone wrong, but that they could have gone so much better. What, then, is the evidence that failure has occurred at all? It is the gap between what was actually achieved and what would have been possible. We simply don't see "the path not taken". But we can get an idea of that missed opportunity by comparing what happened with the achievements of others who managed strategy better, either in the same industry or in similar ones.

Starbucks has a competitor in the UK: Costa Coffee. In 1995, the company had 41 stores, and out-traded Starbucks by one third in like-for-like locations. According to consumer research at the time, this was due to a better offering of food products, a better service experience, and higher consumer preference for its coffee. The company was backed by the vast resources of the large restaurant and hotel group Whitbread PLC, which included the most powerful real-estate development team in the industry. At the time, Starbucks was an ambitious new entrant to the UK, committed to rapid expansion, but Costa could have nailed them, beating them to the best locations and taking leadership of the UK and wider European market. Yet by 1999, the company had grown to just 134 units, leaving Starbucks free to build a strong business in the UK, just as had done in other countries. Costa eventually started moving, growing to 430 stores by 2006, and some 1600 by 2010, many outside the UK. But the company is a shadow of what it could have been, had it exploited its initial advantage by opening up prime store locations before Starbucks had the chance.

Who needs people?

Like strategy successes, mistakes are not limited to the market-facing front end of the business. In 2005, oil giant Shell announced plans to hire 1000 experienced oil engineers. It had just fallen foul of the US Securities and Exchange Commission for misreporting its oil reserves, a mistake caused in large part by a critical staff shortage. This number is equal to about three years' worth of the graduate output of petroleum engineers from the entire US university system! Moreover, comments from other industry players at the time made clear that they were all pretty much in the same mess: short of experienced engineers, and with too few youngsters coming through to fill the gap.

Now, if you are short of experienced engineers in 2005, when did you not hire them? If we consider "experienced" to mean about 10 years in the industry, then you didn't hire them in 1995. So here is an entire

18

industry paying the price for a collective mistake made a decade earlier. And it's not as though this sort of situation isn't foreseeable. There may be many uncertainties in this world, but the fact that people get older each year is not one of them. Everyone involved should have known how many people would be retiring from the far end of the career ladder, and at least considered that replacing them might be useful.

This pernicious mistake has been made in other sectors, as well. During the late 1980s and into the 1990s, the power industry in many countries was privatised, exposing management to pressure from the financial markets to deliver strong returns to new shareholders. A widespread strategy for achieving this was downsizing (or "getting rid of people you need", as it should properly be named). The destruction of career prospects and reduced hiring in the industry was so severe that university programmes in electrical engineering closed down in huge numbers. Those that did not close filled themselves up with keen young things from emerging economies, who on graduation promptly turned around and headed back to where they would be wanted and valued.

Finally, one company, RWE Energie, who operates the power network in the western part of Germany, recognised that its network assets were degrading to the point where the lights could go out. It tried to initiate a large capital investment program to fix the problem, but found it didn't have the people with the necessary capability. Unfortunately, its equipment suppliers couldn't help either, because their experienced staff base had been shredded, too, when the industry stopped investing. Realising that much of the industry's workforce was headed for retirement homes, RWE pulled the emergency-response switch and approached a number of universities, sponsoring the start-up of new degree programmes and guaranteeing employment to the hundreds of new graduates from those programmes.

We should have hired sooner...

If there's one quality that we might expect in the strategic management of a business, surely it's the ability to look just a little further ahead than next quarter's results and ask what could go wrong. Commentators talk about the 2008 recession that "no one saw coming", but as we have seen, management themselves caused that recession, and a few wise teams prepared for the problems that they knew their colleagues were about to visit upon them. On February 1st, 2008, the Netherlands' newspaper Het Financieele Dagblad reported that the country's Rabobank Group "…has taken precautionary measures to secure sufficient liquidity in times of crisis. Late last year, the bank got 30 billion Euro in mortgages ready as a security for loans of the European Central Bank in case of emergency." According to CFO Bert Bruggink, Rabobank had not suffered from the crisis up until then, but wanted to be ready for worse times in the future. "We anticipate on a worst case scenario. I do not assume that we will need it, but at least we are prepared."[12]

The ugly

We need not spend long on this, the worst category of strategic failures. There are plenty more examples, and plenty of information and opinion about them, simply because of their scale and public visibility. But details on a couple of the cases from the Introduction will offer sufficient additional insight.

Swissair was seen by the proud Swiss nation as more than just an airline: it was symbolic of the excellence that pervaded the country's business sector. So the grounding of its fleet in 2001 came as a shock to the entire nation[13]. All had been well until the early 1990s, when consultants McKinsey & Company recommended that the company embark on a "hunter" strategy of buying up poor-quality airlines around Europe, sorting them out with some high-quality Swiss management, and so step up into the big league of international airlines. The company acquired stakes in a dozen airlines, some small, but others larger, such as the loss-making Belgian airline Sabena and Portugal's TAP. All this cost vast amounts of cash, leaving the company crippled with debt. The logic of the strategy might have been reasonable enough, but when embarking on something on such a large scale that neither you nor anyone else has attempted before, you might at least expect to test the process on a small scale first, then learn and scale-up, rather than just betting the farm on its working.

In a quite different context, the global satellite phone company Iridium, backed by Motorola, filed for bankruptcy in 1999 after spending $5 billion to build an infrastructure of 66 satellites to provide a worldwide wireless phone service. The perceived opportunity was clear: a phone service for people who needed availability anywhere on the planet, delivered by launching enough satellites to give global coverage and selling special handsets that could send and receive signals with those satellites. These would then be routed into regular phone networks.

Unfortunately, although some need this universal coverage, for example, those in the oil industry, outside broadcasters, or extreme adventurers, the number of potential customers was very small. By 1999, the company had only 10,000 subscribers, against an anticipated number of half a million. How come? Well, for the business ever to be profitable on its huge cost-base, the service had to capture large numbers of subscribers, but at a high price: an Iridium handset cost $3000 and talk time was as much as $5 a minute. There were also basic limitations to the technology. Because the service depended on line-of-sight between the phone antenna and the orbiting satellite, subscribers were unable to use the phones inside moving cars, in buildings, and in many urban areas.

These limitations and the high cost made it impossible to capture the large numbers of customers on which Iridium's prospects depended. Could costs have been cut and prices therefore made more affordable? Unfortunately, to cut unit costs for any kind of consumer electronic requires substantial manufacturing volume, both to drive costs out through experience-curve effects and to give economies of scale. If you don't get that volume, you can't make your product cheaper, which in turn means you can't grow the volume. Iridium thus found itself in this chicken-and-egg situation, with neither chicken nor egg to get it started.

Meanwhile, Iridium ignored the impact of a powerfully developing substitute: the increasingly widespread and affordable coverage by cell phone networks, of which its major backer Motorola must have been acutely aware. Even a basic analysis would have shown the trajectory of cost and functionality of cell phone services progressing so fast that they would soon be universally affordable in large economies and widely so in developing countries. Granted, they may not be so great for

Antarctic explorers, but for virtually everyone else, coverage was rapidly becoming completely adequate.

Should Iridium have anticipated this? It is a fundamental requirement of professional strategy to look over the horizon and anticipate changes that either open up opportunities or threaten your future. The penetration rate of cell phone networks and its price dynamics were entirely foreseeable and should have challenged the feasibility of the entire Iridium initiative, long before they got to the point of writing off $1.5 billion, making it one of the 20 largest bankruptcies in US history up to that time.

An interesting postscript to this case is that Iridium's assets were subsequently bought up at a knock-down price, enabling the creation of a new business, also called Iridium, that *could* be viable. By 2008 the new company had 300,000 subscribers and made $108 million in profits— nice enough, but never sufficient to have justified the original investment.

The modern corporation: A comfortable home for the psychopath?

A curious question arises from the worst strategy cases: why do teams of intelligent people persist in strategic lunacy, in the face of both their own realisation and mounting evidence that their strategies are failing?

The field of organisational behaviour has much to say about how individuals and teams can become ever more committed to a bold plan, and increasingly reluctant to reverse it—a specific manifestation of the psychological phenomenon of cognitive dissonance, the discomfort caused by simultaneously holding conflicting beliefs[14]. But another intriguing possibility may be at work in some cases.

In September 2011, the BBC's Horizon programme[15] hinted that corporate leadership may feature four times more psychopaths than the average population—up to one in 2515[16]. The programme reviewed basic findings about the cause of psychopathy, that is, a gene malfunction disabling a specific brain function, resulting in a lack of empathy and the need for thrills. It was discussed that, while some psychopaths become killers, most don't, thanks to a nurturing upbringing by loving parents. So most psychopaths are not killers but are actually all around us: they blend in just fine by mimicking the behaviours of others while not caring about them at all.

Then, as a program contributor said, "What better environment for the psychopath than the modern corporation" where they can charm, manipulate, lie, cheat, intimidate, and defy reasoned argument to get their way and make the big plays they need to satisfy their need for thrills? Some of these plays might come off, but there is an equal, if not greater, chance that they might end up destroying the business and its people's well-being. In one case study, half of colleagues surveyed thought the person in question was a great boss—the essence of the charismatic leader, while the other half thought him the devil incarnate.

The last piece is bad news: while these characters featured high on charisma, their actual performance was lousy, both as team players (they are hugely divisive) and in delivering performance. Maybe we need checks to make psychopaths are not leading our corporations to destruction? Just maybe the banking crisis need not have happened?

This chapter has given some brief examples of the problems that can arise when organisations' strategies are faulty, and has contrasted them with cases of better strategic management. Plenty more can be found[17]. See, for example, Richard Rumelt, R. 2011,. Good Strategy: Bad Strategy: The Difference and Why It Matters,. Profile Books. New York: Crown Business." on page 25 [17]. Each has illustrated failure in one or more of the three elements of strategic management identified at the beginning of the chapter: inappropriate objectives, nonsensical strategic positioning, or the poor steering of strategy over time, whether continuous or through acquisition.

Next we need to clarify what exactly it is about the practice of strategic management that makes it the culprit for such failures, rather than poor leadership, ineffective operating procedures, poor financial discipline, or sheer bad luck—and why this situation has persisted for so long.

TIPS

- Check for mistakes others have made before you, especially in your own industry.

- If business conditions look too good to be true, they probably are. Continually check that you will be OK if things get worse.

- If it feels like you are galloping forward with a herd of other wildebeest, do check you are not all heading for a cliff edge.

- Make sure your growth is quality, not just quantity, whether grabbing more customers, launching new products, or adding capacity.

- Be aware of the trajectory of important external changes, not only in order to ensure your business's rationale does not become obsolete, but also to identify circumstances that offer opportunities.

- When making strategy based upon the assumption of changed customer behaviour, do test whether your customers are likely to make that change before betting the business on it.

- Don't forget the supply side of the business. Look for where your policies and industry developments could take things over the long term and make plans to sustain critical resources.

- … and if any of this means you are not going to do the same stupid things as others, in spite of urgings by consultants, bankers, analysts, and the media, tell them why!

Notes

1. Gus Lubin, 2010, "Check Out These Collector's Edition Analyst Reports Calling Lehman A Great Buy", Business Insider, August 4. Retrieved 28-3-2012.

2. Jim Collins, 2001, Good to Great: Why Some Companies Make the Leap...and Others Don't, New York: Random House

3. Steve Hodson, 2010, "Skype Commands 13 Per Cent of International Phone Calls", The Inquistr, May 3. Retrieved 28-3-2012.

4. See the Infosys 2008 Annual Report. Retrieved 28-3-2012.

5. Skype S.à r.l., 2010, IPO Registration Statement, 9th August. Retrieved 28-3-2012.

6. "Blue Ocean" strategy describes the search for new competitive positions that other companies cannot serve, in contrast to the "red ocean" of intensely competitive industries. See Chan Kim and Renée Mauborgne, 2005, Blue Ocean Strategy, Boston: Harvard Business School Press.

7. Mark Perry, 2010, "Due North: Canada's Marvelous Mortgage and Banking System", Journal of the American Enterprise Institute, 26th February. Retrieved 28-3-2012.

8. Giovanni Caveti, Rebecca Henderson, and Simona Giorgi, 2004, Kodak (case study), Boston: Harvard Business School.

9. Thomas J. Peters and Robert H. Waterman, Jr., 1982, In Search of Excellence: Lessons from America's Best-Run Companies, New York: Harper & Row, Publishers, Inc.

10. http://www.independent.co.uk/news/business/analysis-and-features/british-retailers-going-global-744882.html

11. http://www.economist.com/blogs/schumpeter/2011/10/netflix?fsrc=nlw | wwb | 10-13-2011 | business_this_week

12. See Paul de Ruijter, 2010, Rabobank and Scenario Planning. 1st November. Retrieved 5-4-2012.

13. BBC News, 2001, A Nation in Shock: Swissair Crisis, 28th November. Retrieved 28-3-2012.

14. For a readable explanation of this concept and its consequences for poor decision making, see Carol Tavris and Elliot Aronson, 2007, Mistakes Were Made (but Not by Me): Why We Justify Foolish Beliefs, Bad Decisions, and Hurtful Acts, Orlando, FL: Harcourt Books.

15. http://www.bbc.co.uk/programmes/b014kj65

16. See Nick Collins, 2011, "One in 25 business leaders 'could be a psychopath'", Daily Telegraph, 2nd September. Retrieved 28-3-2012.

17. See, for example, Richard Rumelt, R. 2011,. Good Strategy: Bad Strategy: The Difference and Why It Matters,. Profile Books. New York: Crown Business.

CHAPTER TWO

TRUE PROFESSIONALISM

"What is the philosophical foundation of the enterprise? That the most competent, the most able, the most audacious will triumph."

Fidel Castro

Cuba's long-serving communist leader is known for many things, but admiration for professional management would seem a surprising item in his résumé. Yet even Fidel Castro recognizes that to succeed, managers must possess a basic level of competence.

But it is not at all clear what exactly professional competence in strategic management means. So what does being professional look like in other fields? It is no accident that professions instil confidence in those who rely on their services: they exhibit a range of features to ensure that their practitioners know what they are doing and that they will do it well. They can't offer a cast-iron guarantee, of course. Incompetent or dishonest people can worm their way through the tightest controls, but at least we can spot a fool or a rogue when they do.

We can start by considering some of the most rigorous professions, those with a strong base in the physical sciences. You may well object that business isn't like science, that it's way too messy. But we will also see that other professions, operating in equally messy domains, share some characteristics with the science-based professions.

Professionals speak a common, defined language

When your physician says that you have appendicitis, he does not mean that you have some vague stomach pain. He means that the appendix in your lower abdomen is swollen and liable to burst, resulting in peritonitis. When engineers talk about stress, they mean the load per unit of area to which a component is subjected. They don't mean whether or not the load looks a bit much for the component to bear in some vague way.

The term *appendicitis* has been used by physicians for decades with no substantial change in its meaning. It has not been dropped in favour of something that sounds more exciting, nor have individual physicians invented their own words for this complaint. Any medical practitioner understands instantly from the term what is wrong with you and how to fix it. The term *stress* has been used by engineers for centuries. Its definition hasn't changed, and it remains as critical to their work today as when Robert Hooke defined how it affects materials back in 1660.

To be sure, medicine, engineering, and other professions develop as more is learned, and as more complex challenges are tackled. New terms *have* to be added from time to time so that professionals can keep extending their mastery to the constant stream of new challenges we expect them to tackle. But new vocabulary is added only after careful, expert scrutiny, and builds on what is already accepted.

So it seems that a shared and well-defined vocabulary is important if professionals are to be able to perform consistently well, and be seen to do so by those they serve. How, then, does the strategy profession look in terms of this feature? Hopeless. It has no standard terms that mean the same to everyone.

Pick a word — any word

You would think we could at least recognize success when we see it. It seems not. The word "performance" is liberally scattered through the books and articles on the topic of strategy, but when you look closely, it's not at all clear what the term means. Sometimes it refers to profitability — possibly return on sales or maybe return on invested capital; then again, it could be growth, market share, or total returns to shareholders. Writers can't even agree on what the word "strategy" means. I have given one simple definition at the beginning of this book, but you will find nearly as many alternative definitions as there are authors who write them.

When we get into the subject of success itself, we find that people talk about "competitive advantage", "strategic innovation", and a host of other concepts whilst rarely being clear about what they actually mean. If you do not believe me, simply search any strategy term on the Web and watch out for the tidal wave of overblown consulting hype and journalistic fluff that will flood back at you.

Even when the original author does take the trouble to specify their terms, this clarity is quickly thrown aside as others grab a sexy headline and throw it around in all directions. "Core Competence", for example, was clearly defined by C. K. Prahalad and Gary Hamel as a particular feature of large, multi-business corporations who can exploit underlying technologies across multiple product types and end markets[1]. Most people who use the term now, though, take it to mean merely "something we think we are pretty good at" (often, regrettably, with no clear specification of what that something actually is, or any evidence at all that they are indeed pretty good at it)!

Things are even worse in the case of public services and not-for-profit organisations, who operate without the primary financial purpose of commercial businesses. In these cases, the strategy field seems to have given up entirely, offering no clear idea of what success means or how to measure it, let alone how to achieve it.

The latest fad in the academic corner of the field is the so-called resource-based view or RBV as it is affectionately known. Now everyone throws the word "resources" around quite liberally, in the real world as well as in the academic journals. We have surely heard people say "I need more resources to do this" or "That plan was under-resourced", but what people most often actually mean is cash and people. But that's not what the RBV theory means by the term—it focuses only on abstract, intangible things like reputation or human capital.

It really is not good enough to hold up our hands in surrender, on the basis that organisations are just too subtle and complicated for us to be clear and unambiguous in our language. Clear terminology has penetrated other aspects of management, such as production and logistics, of course, where engineering principles are most clearly relevant, but also finance and accounting. Where there remains some room for different interpretations of terms, like "profit", we don't simply give up and leave everyone to make up what they like; we set standard meanings and expect people to clarify exactly how they have treated the uncertainties according to those meanings.

Such clear terminology is a pre-requisite for the next feature that makes professions reliable.

Understanding how things work

Professionals don't just share a common vocabulary; they also share an understanding of what causes what. Accountants, engineers, and doctors understand cause and effect in detail. As a result, they know what will result from a given event or decision, across a range of different circumstances. Where does this confidence come from?

In engineering and many other professions, this confidence is provided by a reliable underlying science. Materials science explains why a bridge stays up, while the science of aerodynamics explains what keeps an aircraft in the air. We would, quite reasonably, feel pretty irritated if a plane had crashed because someone had ignored these fundamental principles. Understanding how things work is at the core of being a professional.

Not all professions have scientific foundations, yet are still able to estimate outcomes for a given situation with some confidence. Some rely on a body of custom and practice built up over decades or centuries. The origins of accountancy, for example, can be traced back to the fifth century BC, when Egyptians and Babylonians adopted systems to double-check everything that went in and out of their storehouses. Later, the Italian monk Luca de Pacioli introduced double-entry book-keeping, building on procedures that had been used in the trading cities of northern Italy since the mid-1300s.

The legal profession, too, stands on foundations of principles, practices, and precedents that stretch back far into history. Magna Carta, set out nearly eight hundred years ago, lay the foundations of freedom for the individual against the arbitrary authority of despots, giving momentum to a whole range of legal concepts and practices we still benefit from to this day. So even where no fundamental science is involved, professions can still rely on recognized, reliable relationships amongst the factors with which they work.

The strategy profession, insofar as it can be said to exist at all, has hardly any useful foundation in reliable theory or principles. It doesn't help, of course, to start with language that is abstract and ill-defined. If we aren't clear about the meaning of the terms we use, nor about the outcomes we want to understand or to bring about, we are hardly likely to find reliable relationships between those terms. The nearest we have got to such answers is some *rough* indication from microeconomics of some possible reasons why some companies may achieve somewhat higher returns on sales or on invested capital than others, based on correlation studies. As we will show in Chapter 4, this is neither a useful outcome to understand, nor a credible way to seek that understanding.

In the absence of any reliable and comprehensive structure of cause and effect for a business—how things work—managers get away with claims that their achievements rely on judgement rather than on demonstrable professional expertise. Indeed, many of those who have led us to disaster seem positively proud of this fact. We know this isn't good enough but seem reluctant to try and fix it. As Clayton Christensen and Michael Raynor point out, if you don't know what factors are driving your performance or how they operate, it's tough to know what changes you might make to improve performance[2].

Incremental progress

Professions build new ideas on what is already known. Pushing into new territory, with new and more complex challenges, they extend their vocabulary, and the relationships that explain how things work.

Medics can now treat illnesses that were unthinkably difficult just a few years ago because they have built on what they learned in earlier times. Thanks to the discoveries of Louis Pasteur and others, we can now treat smallpox, malaria, and even AIDS. No longer do doctors transfer their preferences from blistering to leeches to pomanders as fashions swing to and fro. Accountants now have procedures for dealing with goodwill and intangible assets that build on the principles developed by those Babylonian storekeepers discussed earlier.

Serious professions also deploy their bodies of knowledge as a whole, not picking a single tool from the tool box and thinking that it will provide the complete solution. Making an aircraft that flies needs aeronautics, materials science, control systems, and knowledge of a host of other principles. Operating on your dodgy heart requires understanding of blood flow, neuroscience, anaesthesia, and surgical practice.

True professions do not, then, constantly reinvent what they do, throwing out what is known and starting again with completely new concepts. When they come across a new phenomenon that needs to be explained or a new task that needs to be tackled, they start with what is already known and add new knowledge. Where that knowledge is science-based, the knowledge arises through application of the scientific method. Where knowledge is more procedural than scientific, it is distilled from numerous and widespread episodes where new relationships are observed, checked, and codified. Very occasionally, when a fundamental idea is stretched to breaking point, it has to be abandoned and a paradigm shift takes the field on to a new foundation. But such episodes are extremely rare and treated with great care.

What is the record of the strategy profession on building cumulative knowledge? Well, there has been quite some effort over more than half a century to build new insight from the principles of microeconomics, especially in terms of the so-called "SCP paradigm" how the *Structure* of an industry (how many competitors, of what size, with what rates of entry and exit, and so on) drives management *Conduct* (decisions regarding issues such as pricing, marketing, and capacity expansion), and how these factors subsequently affect *Performance*, usually indicated by some measure of return on investment. Unfortunately, this analysis is of limited practical use, because the relationships don't explain very much—especially not much that anyone can act upon. Consequently, the effort has done little to help improve strategic decision making.

Beyond these broad generalities, most concepts in strategy are too imprecise, abstract, and qualitative, and are open to widely varying interpretations. Into this vacuum has flooded a random series of seemingly bright ideas, breezing in and out of fashion like styles of clothing:

"Each season brings a new crop of experts proclaiming that their frameworks—core competencies, customer retention, management ecosystems, strategic intent, time-based competition, total quality management, 'white spaces', managing chaos, value migration—are definitive."[3]

Though some of these concepts and approaches possess a nugget of reliable principles or a grain of usefulness, many make a big deal out of things that are simple, obvious, or common sense, while others offer prescriptions that are unreliable or downright dangerous. Instead of having a reliable set of approaches—that can be deployed as a complementary tool set—managers are left scrambling to keep up with random novelties. No wonder most don't bother. Try asking a large audience of senior managers which strategy methods or principles they understand and use and you will be greeted with a long, embarrassed silence.

It's not their fault. They urgently need what the strategy field has failed to provide: a body of knowledge, organized into a clear taxonomy of principles that are reliable and respected, and which can be deployed collectively to deal with the challenges and opportunities senior managers face every day.

Standard procedures

We have confidence in professionals, not just because they agree on what they are talking about and know how things work, but because when they need to do something, they follow proven procedures. These have been developed over many decades and built on the solid foundations of well-understood mechanisms—and they have been proven, time and again, to *work*!

You would be surprised if two physicians carried out totally different procedures to diagnose and treat some complaint you might have. You would be puzzled if two accounting firms used their own distinctive approaches in putting together your year-end accounts. You would probably be alarmed if two engineers followed different procedures to make sure an aircraft would fly safely. Even the mechanic who fixes your car at the roadside follows a series of simple procedures to pinpoint the cause of your breakdown.

When we seek strategy advice, on the other hand, we can have no such confidence. Indeed, a leader in one of the top strategy consulting houses proudly told me they positively pride themselves on the fact that the advice given to a client will depend on which partner happens to lead the engagement!

If strategy consultancy were being conducted professionally, we should expect to find some standard questions addressed, data gathered, and basic procedures followed to provide sound justification for any findings and recommendations. Strategy consulting firms will tell you that they have such standard procedures, of course. Indeed, some hint at the methods they use on their websites, in their house journals, or in books written by their consultants[4]. However, these descriptions are mostly superficial, and are certainly not laid out in sufficient enough detail to allow public scrutiny of their validity or value. Nor, judging by the strategy course curricula that feature in business school course brochures, are those methods widely taught in public programs to young professionals. Consequently, we have no way of recognizing whether such standard procedures exist, whether they are proven to be reliable, or whether their advisers are following them competently.

This lack of clarity about procedures for strategy is especially damaging because the work clients get from these advisers is not usually carried out by senior folk with extensive experience. The business model for most strategy consulting firms of any significant size relies on hiring bright youngsters, giving them a quick sheep dip in basic analysis skills and access to the firm's knowledge base, then charging them out at high day rates onto costly projects sold by senior partners. In the best cases, this can actually work—where there are clear best practices that have been proven to work. But in too many cases, sophisticated clients become irritated by partners who sell their firm's specialist capability, only to send in busloads of naïve youngsters who understand not even the basics of how the client's business actually works.

How consultants go about developing strategy for their clients is, of course, the source of their high fees. They would look at the auditing profession, where there is virtually no scope for distinctiveness, and shudder at the wafer-thin profit margins that auditors have to tolerate. No surprise, then, that strategy consultants are not keen to lay out in public how exactly they do what they do. But we might ask ourselves why we expect transparency and professionalism in other high-stakes endeavours, but not with strategy consultancy; why we expect proven best practices from other professionals, but not these.

We should perhaps not expect *too* much from standard procedures in strategy. As soon as it becomes clear how one firm is winning through some distinctive strategy, its competitors are likely to copy, adapt, or undermine its approach. Nevertheless, there should be some solid basics to the task, which everyone understands and upon which cake any brilliant insights should be the icing. Widespread knowledge of the basic principles of construction has not stopped Richard Rogers or Tadao Ando rising to the top of their profession. Neither has the universal knowledge of automotive engineering prevented Toyota or BMW creating industry-beating cars.

Safety first

Professional practice is not just about victory. First and foremost, it's about *safety*. Boeing and Airbus are engaged in a battle to achieve superior performance in their aircraft—greater range, better fuel economy, and so on—but they share an even stronger commitment to making sure their planes don't fall out of the sky. For them, "competitive advantage" takes second place to "avoid failure".

Not so in business strategy, where leaders often demonstrate a cavalier disregard for the continuing health of our organisations, a task for which proven best practice should be the guiding principle. Like thousands of other companies that made the same mistake, Starbucks should have known that its over-expansion from 2002–07 was risky, assessed that risk against the possibility, indeed *probability*, that trading conditions might deteriorate, and asked how the business would perform under such conditions. The banks that messed up all our lives in 2008–09 simply forgot to ask the critical question—"What is the worst that can go wrong here?" —a question that has supposedly underpinned the world of banking for as long as banks have existed, and should be tattooed on the forehead of anyone with strategic responsibility for an organisation. Management and consultants alike would do well to observe the simplified exhortation popularly thought to start medicine's Hippocratic oath (though it actually appears later, and in different words): "First, do no harm."

In spite of what has just been said about strategy consultancy, and in spite of the failures for which they are sometimes responsible, embarking on a general campaign of consultant-bashing is neither appropriate nor helpful. Strategy consultants perform valuable functions that it would be foolish to ignore. They develop far more information about markets, industries, and the companies within industries than any but the largest corporations could justify collecting and maintaining for themselves. As a result, any company assessing whether to develop beyond the bounds of their current activity may well find it is quicker and better to seek access to that knowledge than attempt to create it themselves. We just need to be cautious about the capability and potential contribution of strategy consultants.

Learning and standards

Professions train their people! And that training is extensive, demanding, and time-consuming. Just think how long it takes to qualify as a doctor, lawyer, engineer, or accountant. Not only does training give professionals confidence in what they know, it also makes them painfully aware of what they *don't* know. Until they reach the pinnacle of their field (and even then!), they always understand that there is more to be known.

Training alone, however, is not enough—professions need standards. Examinations at varying levels are important to make clear, both to the individual and others, a professional's level of proficiency. Such examinations are public, consistent, and rigorous, and a recognized prerequisite for practising in the field. Failure by those taking examinations is widespread and accepted as a guarantee of standards and, paradoxically, *increases* the appeal of the profession—the harder it is to get in, the more people want to! The nearest that management gets to a qualification is the MBA degree, but in spite of the efforts of accreditation bodies, MBA qualifications lack standards and rigour, and in any case give only fleeting attention to strategy.

It would be nice if we could lay out simple principles for strategic management that leaders could just pick up from a short book or two, but it's not that simple—the task really is complex and ever-changing. Those who claim "it's just common sense" are cruelly deceiving you. In any case, few of those who make such claims have ever actually done the job. Given the need to comprehend standard terms, understand cause and effect, accumulate knowledge and use proven procedures, the only route to professional strategic management is through education and training.

So strategy professionals, too, need training. Unfortunately, as we have seen, the basic foundations for a profession—a common language, known relationships, cumulative knowledge and standard procedures—do not exist. So it is hard to know what exactly such training might consist of.

This lack of effective education, examination, and qualification is disturbing. It is astounding that shareholders are happy for their money and aspirations to be handled by executives with nothing more than some history of happening to make the right judgement calls and excessive self-belief. In what other field would we put our wealth and safety in the hands of individuals who aren't required to offer any evidence of their competence? Your neighbour may be supremely confident in his ability to take out your grumbling appendix, and may have taken a few first-aid classes and bandaged a strained ankle, but he has no surgical training and no qualification for *that* specific task. You and your appendix would run a mile!

Policing the professions

The last feature of true professions that deserves comment is the role of professional associations and institutions. These bodies develop and protect standards for their fields and oversee the training and probity of their practitioners. Consider the US American Institute of Certified Public Accountants (AICPA)5: with 330,000 members, it is the premier professional association for accountants. Its website explains in considerable detail what the AICPA does, and how, and includes this mission statement:

> "... to provide members with the resources, information, and leadership that enable them to provide valuable services in the highest professional manner to benefit the public as well as employers and clients."

To achieve its mission, the AICPA has some priorities, including:

- seeking the highest possible level of uniform certification and licensing standards

- promoting public awareness and confidence in the integrity, objectivity, competence, and professionalism of CPAs

- encouraging highly qualified individuals to become CPAs

- supporting the development of outstanding academic programs

- establishing professional standards

- assisting members in continually improving their professional conduct, performance, and expertise

- monitoring such performance to enforce professional standards[6].

This profession is clearly not flip-flopping in the wind, changing its aims on a whim. The AICPA has a rock-solid, long-term purpose, and is clearly focused on achieving this, building on its solid achievements to date. The practice of strategic management can only dream of such rigour!

How professional is strategy?

In our field, a mountain of statistical studies has found only the flimsiest relationship between success (most often poorly defined) and its putative causes. We have failed to build cumulative knowledge, so organisations lurch from one fad to another, one moment obsessed with industry forces, then scenario planning, then core competences, then transformation. "Thought leadership" is what counts for the consultants—as if a thought is preferable to a rigorous analysis of information, leading to sound conclusions and effective actions.

Management make virtually no use of any formal approaches to develop strategy or to make strategically critical decisions. Instead, they display a horrifying tendency to follow simplistic recipes or to copy others, pursuing the strategies of admired peers and being surprised when they fall off the same cliff. Surely, by the twenty-first century, we might expect professionals to use reliable tools and techniques when they are responsible for creating our wealth.

So long as this unacceptable situation persists, we are vulnerable to flawed advice—or even deception. With no reliable terminology or proven relationships, strategy has become the subject of journalism, not professionalism. Writers take no care in their language, often inventing or redefining terms to suit a particular agenda. We could pick hundreds of examples to illustrate the point, but consider just one such journalistic contribution, on the current fad of strategic transformation[7]. This article describes how Netflix, the strongest provider of movies-by-post, "redefined its business model" by offering streaming video—hardly a move of strategic genius—and how a provider of wedding services "transformed: itself by focusing on a particular niche of the market. Both examples are completely trivial but are apparently sufficient to prove that "...the era of disciplined expansion is dead." Tell that to Toyota, IKEA, or drinks producer SAB-Miller.

So just how much damage can the pursuit of fads, sold by consultants, actually be? Consider this description of Bank of America in the 1980s:

> "[The company] *tried to pull off its own version of Mao's Cultural Revolution by hiring corporate change consultants who led 'corporate encounter groups' and tried to institute a 'rah-rah approach to management.' Lurched after Charles Schwab; culture clash erupted, and later sold it back. Lurched after Security Pacific, trying to emulate Wells Fargo's Crocker merger; acquisition failed, creating a multibillion-dollar write-off."[8]*

In engineering or medicine, similar levels of failure would be unthinkable. If the poor professionalism in strategy took place in accounting, we would see huge financial trouble, leading to an immediate outcry and calls that "something must be done." The fact that poor strategic management (mostly) doesn't put lives at risk or immediately destroy companies doesn't mean that we should tolerate its weaknesses. It is curious indeed that for the most critical role of the most senior executives in our most important organisations, we are content to shrug our shoulders and just hope the next candidate who walks through the door can do better.

The damage caused by such amateurism is unacceptable. Wealth is destroyed, customers are disappointed, investors are impoverished, and employees lose their careers. All of these things will happen anyway in the normal course of free enterprise, so why increase their likelihood with poor advice and execution?

Clearly, many people—employees, shareholders, and customers—would benefit from greater management professionalism. Perhaps, then, the current situation of poor strategic management continues because those currently holding sway are the potential losers (consultants, leadership personalities, and academics) were things to change; they have a strong incentive to reject any suggestion that strategy is a trainable skill. These groups prefer to maintain that strategy is a black art, even more complex and impenetrable than medicine or engineering, say. Such mystification enables them to promote new fashions and sustain the constant activity that results from each new fad.

We have established that reliable methods and procedures are central to professional practice. In the next chapter, we will take a look at some of the strategy tools available to management and assess how effective they may be.

The finance take-over

Nature abhors a vacuum, and into the strategy vacuum, Finance has stepped. CEOs and investors need *some* idea of future performance (specifically, a cash flow forecast), and *some* idea of how it will be delivered. And since Strategy has had nothing to say on the subject (no strategy textbook or article explains how to get a cash flow forecast out of the methods it describes), they have turned to the only group who does have a perspective on the whole organisation and seems to have a view: Finance.

Now Finance has serious and important responsibilities and plays a critical role in keeping the show on the road, but they don't understand strategy. No amount of scrutiny of revenue growth, margins, cost ratios, return on capital, or debt/equity ratios is going to tell you anything about how market development, competitor behaviour, or other external factors may affect your organisation's future. But that doesn't stop Finance thinking it can do the job. Here's a summary of how one major reference book in the field (and in other respects an outstanding text that should be on every strategist's bookshelf!) says performance forecasting should be done:[9]

> **Step 1: Prepare and Analyse Historical Financials** by collecting financial information, entering it into a spreadsheet, and building

a set of financial statements: income statement, balance sheet, and cash flow. *(It's not clear what analysis might be helpful in forecasting future performance, but one suspects it's a set of trend and ratio calculations.)*

Step 2: Build the Revenue Forecast. This should combine a top-down approach, using forecasts for market growth, market share, and prices, as well as a bottom-up approach looking at customer growth and purchase rate. Basing these forecasts on the company's announced plans is recommended, Starbucks' future store openings, or an oil company's oil reserve development plans, for example.

Step 3: Forecast the Income Statement. Decide what economic relationships drive the line items, because most line items are tied directly to revenue *(why?)*. Estimate the forecast ratio for each line item, then multiply the forecast ratio by its driver, usually revenue. *(To translate, for example, if an airline's staff cost has been 12 percent of revenue and you think it can be brought down to 11 percent, multiply your revenue forecast by this changing ratio to get a labour cost forecast).*

Steps 4-5 then explain how to forecast the balance sheet.

Not a word about assessing the market and competitive environment, or estimating the resources (properly defined) to drive success, safely, in that environment. The book could have at least recommended that these tasks be done and pointed to other sources of sound advice for doing so. Instead, it implies that forecasting business performance starts and ends with crude trends and financial ratios. And that, so often, is just what gets done.

The whole notion of forecast-based strategy is flawed in any case. Successful organisations do not so much forecast the future as create it. The world is the way it is today because Microsoft, Apple, IKEA, Skype, Google, Tata Steel, SAP, BMW, and hundreds of other great organisations have made it like this, not because some divine authority has ordained that "The market for product X will grow at 5 percent per year!"

So extensively has the corporate world bought in to the idea that performance is all about financial forecasts, targets, and controls that a finance background is seen as a great qualification to be CEO, rather than, say, having actually run the operations of the business. As of 2010, fully half of FTSE 100 company CEOs had a background in finance or banking[10].

A strategy based on financial trends, ratios, and targets creates two strangely contrasting dangers, both of which are evident in cases of failure and underperformance (that is, failure to deliver potential, sustainable cash flow growth):

> **It strangles business development.** If you think your job is to attain and sustain a high rate of return on invested capital, then pressing down on cost ratios is where you will focus. Surely you don't need all that training and marketing expenditure, and just look how much profit margin customer service is sucking up! With this line of thinking, you might also under-invest in capital (remember how the utilities cut back?).
>
> **It INCREASES exposure to risk.** This is really quite ironic, given that Finance's major responsibility is to protect the business against failure.

To expand on the second point, Finance-driven strategy gets you in trouble on both of the main steps of forecasting (see steps 2 and 3 above): growing revenue and squeezing costs. With the CFO breathing down your neck to deliver revenue growth, you may well try to expand, get into new markets, or launch new products, even when the quality of that expansion would be poor (remember the Starbucks stores?). In extreme cases, you could well over-extend on just about everything. A personal finance company I helped dig out of a mess a few years back had done the lot: dozens of investment funds that were not selling, too many inexperienced analysts working on valueless tasks, brokers with few, poor-quality clients, and policy-holders with too little wealth to be worth serving.

On the costs side of the business, if you have long under-spent on critical revenue and capital items like people, customer support, or physical assets, what happens when trading conditions get difficult or your overly optimistic growth plans start to wobble? You don't have the slack to fix things. To make matters worse, Finance will then likely say, "We have to cut costs," — often a simple across-the-board percentage, which can't possibly, ever be the right answer! So not only does the business not have the capacity to recover, it cuts back still further. The solution if we are losing the race, it seems, is to hack off our legs so we have less weight to carry! No wonder it has taken so long to recover from the 2008 recession, with emaciated corporations wilting by the roadside.

A continual, obsessive focus on profitability and cost ratios, then, clearly has the potential to both strangle and destroy a business—but let's not get silly about this. Of course it is important for the business to be profitable enough that it can invest in its own development and can cover the cost of any external money it may need to raise. And of course, if cash is bleeding so fast that bankruptcy is imminent, the haemorrhaging has to be stopped. But in too many cases Finance has been allowed to go much further and disable the strategic health of corporations. Worse still, the analysts who pronounce on corporate performance have jumped on the same bandwagon, slamming companies they view as inefficient and praising those who deliver unsustainable growth and profitability.

TIPS

Here are some practical lessons arising from this chapter for anyone working on strategy, whether as part of the responsible team or as an adviser.

- Don't even start discussing strategy until everyone involved is crystal-clear about what exactly is meant by the words you will all be using.

- There's no point trading opinions about what drives performance or what choices should be made when there is no evidence that the causality being claimed is real. So what does the data say?

- If anyone claims that a particular strategy method or approach is useful, ask them to specify exactly how it works: what information is needed, what you do with it, what questions it answers, and what decisions it may then inform. Then ask for worked examples of cases where the strategy method has been successfully applied.

- When hiring someone for strategy work, whether internally or as a consultant, ask them what qualifications they have, what methods they use, and—again—ask for worked examples of success.

- And lastly, don't let Finance lead your strategy.

Notes

1. C. K. Prahalad and G. Hamel, 1990, "The Core Competence of the Corporation", Harvard Business Review, May–June, pp. 79–91.
2. Clayton Christensen and Michael Raynor, 2003, "Why Hard-Nosed Executive Should Care About Management Theory", Harvard Business Review, September, pp. 66–74.
3. Kevin Coyne and Somu Subramaniam, 2000, "Bringing Discipline to Strategy", The McKinsey Quarterly Strategy Anthology. Retrieved 28-3-2012.
4. See, for example, The McKinsey Quarterly, Booz & Company's strategy+business, and Carl W. Stern and Michael S. Deimler, Eds., 2006, The Boston Consulting Group on Strategy: Classic Concepts and New Perspectives, Hoboken, NJ: John Wiley & Sons, Inc.
5. The American Institute of Certified Public Accountants (AICPA) can be found at http://www.aicpa.org/
6. AICPA Activities & Major Programs, www.aicpa.org/About/MissionandHistory/Pages/majorprograms.aspx. Retrieved 23-4-2012.
7. Scott Anthony, 2010, "Constant Transformation Is the New Normal", Harvard Business Review Blog, 27th October. Retrieved 28-3-2012.
8. Gary Hector, 1988, Breaking the Bank: The Decline of Bankamerica, New York: Little, Brown and Company.
9. Tim Koller, Marc Goedhart, and David Wessels, 2010, Valuation: Measuring and Managing the Value of Companies, Fifth Edition, Hoboken, NJ: John Wiley & Sons, Inc., pp. 188–206.
10. Richard Young, 2012, "CFO to CEO – Is It Really for You?", CFO World, 30th March. Retrieved 20-3-2012.

CHAPTER THREE

TOOLS, WHAT TOOLS?

When you can measure what you are speaking about, and express it in numbers, you know something about it; but when you cannot measure it, when you cannot express it in numbers, your knowledge is of a meagre and unsatisfactory kind.

Lord Kelvin

Before diving into this chapter, I must first offer an apology. It is not possible to explain the failures of strategy without demonstrating weaknesses in the principles, methods, approaches, and frameworks. And it is not possible to do that without implicitly criticizing those who have developed and promoted those ideas.

I do not mean to imply that those individuals are foolish or motivated by any less than the best of intentions. They are no doubt thoughtful, intelligent, and committed people, genuinely trying to produce ideas that are useful. Unfortunately, it is only too easy for large numbers of people, all striving to do good, to end up collectively doing quite the opposite, for reasons that will be explained.

Incidentally, I make no apology that this chapter reflects on some pretty old strategy approaches as well as more recent developments. We've already pointed out that any decent profession makes use of tools that were proven decades or even centuries ago, and as we will see, what managers think of as strategy today still includes many old methods.

What do executives use?

Many managers don't do strategy at all; they don't develop a coherent plan that is soundly based on what is happening within and around their organisation, keep adapting that plan as events unfold, or steer their decision making according to the plan[1]. People go on about how the world is so dynamic and uncertain that planning is pointless, even dangerous, but that's plain wrong. Even in the most fast-moving of environments, the best-run companies don't take turbulence to mean they should have no strategy; the very best use that dynamism to create the future they want.

It is hardly news that the practice of strategy is patchy at best. One of many such investigations reported the following:

- Seventy-five percent of executive teams did not have a clear customer proposition.

- Less than 5 percent of a typical organisation's workforce understood the organisation's strategy.

- Only 51 percent of senior managers, 21 percent of middle managers, and 7 percent of line employees had personal goals linked to their organisation's strategy.

- Up to 25 percent of strategy measures changed each year[2].

To be sure, management teams have strategy *debates* and strategy *meetings*, or if they are really serious about it, strategy *retreats*. They may even write what they call strategic *plans*, but most of these contain little factual evidence, except for basic financials, and nothing resembling professional analysis, reliable conclusions, or well-founded, coherent choices across all parts of the business. The documents they create often start with some generalized discussion about changes in the marketplace and go on to announce bold intentions to achieve market leadership or build core competences. Most end up as little more than three-year budgets that, following the finance-driven approach discussed in Chapter 2, begin with a market forecast, inexplicable intentions to win market share, and aggressive aspirations to cut cost ratios.

Many organisations, it seems, have no idea where they are going or how to get there, and keep their underlings in the dark. Why is that? They wouldn't dream of having no financial budget, no plans for marketing, or no product development plan, so why is it acceptable to have no solid sense of where the business as a whole is going? Talking with executives, they seem to be well aware that they *ought* to have a clear direction and strategy, but they just don't know how. And the fact that they don't know *how* is not their fault. It's the fault of the strategy profession, such as it is, for not providing the tools for the job.

This chapter, then, looks at some of the common tools, techniques, and methods that managers can use to develop and manage their organisation's strategy. This discussion will show the muddle-headed notions upon which such tools are based and highlight how hopelessly irrelevant many tools are to the real strategic challenges that managers face. The examples that follow were chosen because they are typical of the most common strategy approaches; they are by no means the worst that can be found, nor is this summary intended to single out particular individuals for criticism.

What gets done?

Try this. Take any diverse audience of senior managers: people who are part of management teams responsible for substantial businesses or business units within large corporations. Then ask them how they go about strategy and what methods they use.

After an embarrassed silence, some brave soul might say they use SWOT analysis: an assessment of their organisation's strengths, weaknesses, opportunities, and threats, often in the form of four lists of bullet points. Others will then nod sheepishly in agreement. Ask them exactly what this approach entails, and you're likely to get as many answers as there are people in the audience. If your senior managers include any recent MBA graduates, they may add that they do market segmentation (distinguishing different groups of customers) or value-chain analysis (working out margins and cost ratios). More sophisticated folk may claim to do scenario planning, but probe what that involves and you will likely discover that they consider best-case and worst-case forecasts for their market and then work out best-case and worst-case forecasts for their business.

To back up the anecdotal impression that managers don't do strategy, we can offer further support. The management consultancy firm Bain & Company has for many years surveyed senior managers about which tools they use[3]. The survey covers 25 common tools, selected for being relevant to senior management, topical, and measurable. The list, though, is a curious mix of processes that people think they ought to do, like "strategic planning" and "growth strategies"; things people think they ought to have, like "Mission and Vision Statements"; and a wide range of actions that might usefully feature in a strategy, such as outsourcing, mergers and acquisitions, knowledge management, and collaborative innovation.

The list is almost completely devoid of any genuine tools for working out which strategy to pursue or clarifying how to do it. The Balanced Scorecard (BSC) approach was listed as the sixth most common tool in use in the 2011 report. While this is a valuable approach, and a big step forward from the crude financial ratio controls that are still common, it has major limitations; it makes no mention of the company's market or competitors, for example. To judge by this and other items on the list, you would hardly imagine that competition exists at all. The only half-way professional strategy approach that features in the 2011 survey is scenario planning, though as we have noted, this approach often involves little more than best/worst forecasts[4].

Previous surveys did at least include (albeit near the bottom) two methodologically respectable approaches: value chain analysis and the so-called Five Forces Framework from Harvard professor Michael Porter[5]. But by the 2009 survey, even these two had disappeared. Perhaps most depressing, the executives surveyed reported a 30-percent drop during 2008 in their use of any formal methods at all, as they resorted to crude cost-cutting. And by the time you get to number 25 on the 2011 list ("decision rights tools", whatever they might be and however they may contribute to strategy), usage has dropped to just 10 percent of survey respondents.

Now, you may argue that your average manager is busy running things from day to day and can't be expected to worry about strategy. But bear in mind that Bain is largely surveying the more senior levels of management: the very people for whom strategy is the major responsibility. And as noted in our Introduction, organisations no longer operate by the command-and-control methods of the past, where decisions were made at the top and passed down to middle and junior managers to action. Changes in markets and competitive conditions happen too quickly now for every question to be passed up the chain and every decision to be passed down again. Today, management teams at even quite low levels need the skills and tools to act on their own initiative, which they can only do safely if they have a basic understanding of strategy.

The one bright spot is that most of those surveyed do at least do "strategic planning", though they do not seem to use any formal tools or methods to accomplish this task. A separate survey of top managers by McKinsey & Company found that the strategic planning process performs some useful functions: providing a basis for a more detailed annual budget and deciding where to allocate resources. However, most felt it contributed little to strategy. As one respondent reported, "It is like some primitive tribal ritual. There is a lot of dancing, waving of feathers, and beating of drums. No one is exactly sure why we do it, but there is an almost mystical hope that something good will come out of it."[6]

This is hardly surprising. Strategy can no longer be an annual top-team party, producing plans that stay unchanged until the next anniversary; local management needs to know how to adjust its strategy continually, often from month to month, and how to make strategic choices at any time, across all parts of the business: product development, marketing, human resources, operations, and so on.

To illustrate....One April a few years back, a friend of mine took a job heading a business unit within pharmaceuticals company Glaxo. He was met with a warning of a major new threat from Glaxo's biggest competitor, targeting the division's most important product. The competitor would launch their product before the summer and would aim to take most of my friend's customers before September. In the event, we put together a strategy that destroyed the attack and lost less than 15 percent of the Glaxo product's sales. But consider this: the event never appeared in the business plan or budget for that year (it could not have done because the competitor was hardly going to warn them!), and the issue disappeared before the following year's plan and budget were put together. Strategy has to respond *continually* to changing circumstances, not be locked to a routine cycle.

The bottom line is that most managers, even at top levels, have no professional grasp of strategy and instead follow fads.

49

So what are those executives in the Bain survey missing out on? What are the powerful tools and methods they *could* be using to work out their overall strategy and to inform the strategic decisions they need to continually make to ensure success? Take any strategy textbook from the shelf and you will find methods that fall into a number of broad categories: checklists, option lists, magic bullets, two-by-two boxes, and "frameworks", most of which consist of nothing more than word-and-arrow diagrams. Let's look at some examples of each.

Checklists

Checklists litter the pages of both textbooks and articles aimed at executives. Some describe features of contrasting situations; some tell you what to do in those cases: others list things you should be sure to think about under different circumstances. Of course it is a good idea to make sure you cover all the important considerations in any initiative you take, but most considerations on such lists are self-evident or so vague and generalized as to be meaningless.

So-called SWOT analysis is perhaps the oldest, and, as we have noted, most recognised checklist of all. It does make sense to think about the opportunities and threats in your environment and the strengths and weaknesses of your organisation to deal with them. But in practice, nothing much has changed since a 1997 study that reviewed the use of SWOT analysis by business consultants as part of their approach to understanding the client companies they served. All the cases showed similar characteristics: long lists (consisting of over 40 factors on average), general (often meaningless) descriptions, a failure to prioritize, and no attempt to verify that items listed were indeed strengths, weaknesses, opportunities or threats. But the most worrying finding of the analysis was that no one subsequently used the outputs generated in later stages of the strategy process.

Moving on to more recent ideas, here is a list describing the features of our increasingly hypercompetitive world (note the invention of a fancy-sounding word to make the concept sound important). Rather than pick on any particular source, this list is typical of what can be found in dozens of strategy textbooks:

- No competitive advantage lasts long.

- The ability to break the mould is a core competence.

- Predictability is dangerous; surprise is important.

- Competing makes winning more difficult.

And here's the kind of advice that goes along with that list of features:

- Don't bother sustaining old advantages; it stops you building new ones.

- Beware of attacking competitors' weaknesses.

- There is no point in having an overall strategic plan.

- It is useful to send out misleading competitive signals.

Yeah, right! So to follow this advice, what information should management seek, to work out what answers to what questions, to arrive at what exactly to do on Monday morning?

If checklist strategy is meaningless in the textbooks, it can get positively dangerous when it appears in the popular management journals. Take the following recommendations for how to destroy competitors[7]. This urges management to deploy five strategies "in bursts of ruthless intensity":

- Devastate rivals' profit sanctuaries.

- Plagiarize with pride.

- Deceive the competition.

- Unleash massive and overwhelming force.

- Raise competitors' costs.

Now the article recommending this approach is correct to highlight the competitive strength and commitment of powerful firms like Toyota, Walmart, and Dell. But this simplistic checklist completely trivialises the sophisticated strategic management of these mighty performers. Worse still, it may incite lesser organisations to actually try implementing these recommendations, when they have not the slightest capability to do so. Just imagine the annual strategy conference. The CEO rouses top executives with a stirring rendition of his or her determination to carry out this hardball strategy. The troops leave the event energized and determined to win a huge competitive battle.

Unfortunately, few organisations actually possess the information or skill necessary to work out how to turn these trite phrases into reality. Nor do they have anything like the resources or capability to make it happen. The audience will walk away with only the vaguest idea of what to do. They will initiate a lot of pointless activity using energies that would be better spent ensuring they run their business properly. If they get as far as initiating competitive warfare, they risk burning huge amounts of cash, starting price wars or advertising wars, destroying profitability in their markets, and doing irreparable harm to their reputation with customers.

This is typical of the simplistic, one-size-fits-all answers that pass as serious strategy advice, even from experienced senior figures. It is not the first time management journals have come out with naïve headlines in the guise of serious management advice, nor the first time that management have swallowed it whole and gone on to wreak havoc.

Options Lists

Another form of guidance comes from tools giving people a set of alternatives from which they must *choose*. Cost leadership versus differentiation is the old favourite; you can win, it is said, either by being the lowest-cost supplier or by differentiating what you do so you can charge more. You can't, it is said, do both, and if you try you will end up stuck in the middle and fail. Even though making such a choice does seem to describe how certain companies have succeeded, the idea is now old hat and has been thrown out. (Remember: in strategy, we don't build on what we previously knew). So we have moved on to more sophisticated options lists for choosing an organisation's strategy.

One such list consists of "value disciplines" from which any business must choose:[8]

- *Operational excellence:* superb operations and execution.

- *Product leadership:* very strong in innovation and brand marketing, operating in dynamic markets.

52

- *Customer intimacy:* excelling in customer attention and service.

The management team in an international chemicals firm, who would rather not be named, got hold of this idea and went to work on their two main businesses. After many away days and workshops, they identified that one business needed customer intimacy and the other operational excellence, and decreed that each should pursue its own value discipline consistently and vigorously, as recommended. Senior management spent a couple of years trying to make the approach work before it became apparent that no-one else in the organisation could understand why two businesses that overlapped in so many respects (the underlying technologies, the customers served, and the marketing and distribution channels used to reach the customers) were being kept apart by a crude and arbitrary labelling.

With the help of more consultants, the team discovered that they had actually classified the two activities the wrong way around in any case, and that the classification took no account of the interdependencies upon which the strength of both businesses relied. Fortunately, not too much damage had been done. Management below the top team had decided from the start that none of the strategy made sense and carried on communicating with each other and exploiting opportunities for the two businesses to build off each other.

Another choice management is advised to make is not so much either/or as more/less, that is, how much resource should be devoted to:

- *exploiting* current business activity, or

- *exploring* for new opportunities.

Apparently, this resource allocation is a critical choice that every company's strategy needs to get right. And it's more than just a management checklist: it's a vast field of academic study, asking questions such as how much "knowledge" gets "leveraged" between the two priorities. It is used to assess the most appropriate balance for different types of firms in different contexts.[9]

But the whole notion of resource allocation is built on a flawed fallacy: that there is some finite pot of resources that must be allocated between two purposes. So, for example, and getting a bit more practical than the

53

abstract idea of leveraging knowledge, consider that you have a $100-million research and development (R&D) budget and have to decide how much to spend on improving current products and creating new ones.

However, this is simply the wrong question. What you should be doing:

1. Identify what quantity of resources (people and money) you need to support and exploit your existing core business? (If you do not have enough even for that purpose, then you will have to focus on a smaller set of cash-flow generating activities).

2. If successful, the core business will generate cash flow (and possibly additional people) that you can then use to exploit other, already known, opportunities. If you do not have enough cash flow or people to exploit the opportunities, then you will have to select those that are most attractive (properly defined). **Do not** spread your effort out across all opportunities! You will under-resource them all and most likely fail in them all. If a truly promising opportunity cannot be resourced, then go find some more resources (cash and people), provided you can do so without exposing the core business to unacceptable risk.

3. If you genuinely have no more known opportunities, by all means go exploring for more. List any you find in order of likely value (again, properly defined). Then pick the most promising candidate from the list and deploy any surplus cash and people to that opportunity. Again, if it is necessary and safe, go find any extra resources (cash and people) you need.

The essential principle here is that you put extra resources into exploring new opportunities — you **do not** steal resources from the core business.

This is an example of a rather bizarre but widespread notion, that management's key strategy question is how to "allocate" some fixed quantity of resources. Take a look at the academic research on strategy, and you will find hundreds upon hundreds of studies and papers on resource allocation[10]. The implication is that you have, say, a fixed quantity of money to spend and must share out the pennies between marketing, customer support, IT, and so on. Or you have a finite number of people and must decide how many of them go out selling and how many work on R&D. *(Actually, we can probably guess where the idea of allocation came from — Finance again! You know what revenue you have and what profit margin you want to make, so that tells you what total costs you are allowed to spend, leaving you with the simple task of sharing that out between different functions.)*

The correct approach is to instead ask what *absolute quantity* of people and money are needed to enable each function of the business to perform its role sufficiently to deliver the strategy. This could even be less than you would allocate with Finance's percentage rules. If the resulting total leaves you likely to be unprofitable, then you have to decide whether to invest the resources in any case because they will deliver strong cash flows in later years, or whether not to do some of the things you planned, and cut your performance aims accordingly.

Magic bullets

Some advisers prefer to offer the magic bullet — the single, total solution to all your problems.

Remember the downsizing fashion of the early 1990s? Few executives who followed the advice, the consultants who recommended it, or the analysts who cheered it on, ever knew that this was never a seriously evaluated strategic technique. It was a bit of glib advice from aggressive Wall Street folk, out to make a quick few million bucks. A short summary of the rationale for downsizing was that any firm whose stock trades at a price–earnings (P/E) ratio less than its peers in the same industry is undervalued and therefore badly managed and/or ripe for take-over. It therefore needs to boost earnings, which will be reflected in a disproportionate increase in the stock price (and will thus fix the P/E problem). The quickest way to do this is to slash the single largest cost in most businesses other than raw materials: people.

Jonathan Lurie, of Princeton University, has traced the story of downsizing, asking "why and how managers presented a doom-and-gloom vision to workers (laying them off by the thousands) on one hand, and on the other hand, projecting a rosy view of the corporation to shareholders, so that the stock price would soar."[11] Dr Lurie asks why the powerful industry leaders of the time, such as AT&T, as well as near–basket-cases like Delta Airlines, ever bought into downsizing — or "dumbsizing," as he perhaps more accurately describes it.

Of course we should make sure that we aren't carrying excessive cost, and firms in the kind of predicament Delta faced at the time may need to take tough actions to survive. But that's not what downsizing was about. The concept simply asserted that slashing huge numbers of employees was highly advantageous in and of itself. And the price Delta paid in later years for firing this magic bullet was high. Eliminating 12,000 people from allegedly superfluous roles, such as baggage handling, maintenance, and customer service was not helpful, and the firm continued to flirt with bankruptcy, filing for Chapter 11 protection in 2006. Still, the CEO at the time of this downsizing was lauded for his achievement, featuring as keynote speaker at the 1998 conference of the Strategic Management Society.

The originator of the downsizing idea has since apologized for the damage he caused, though he was not apparently sorry enough to give his wealth back to those who saw their savings, livelihoods, and careers destroyed by his nonsense.

From caterpillar to butterfly

Strategic transformation is a more recent magic bullet, heavily promoted by consultants, academics, and business writers. One consultancy even redefined itself as "transformation advisers". (One wonders what services it would then offer to clients it had already transformed?) Management in business after business was sold the mad idea that what they were doing was bound to be wrong and that they should throw it out, even if it worked fine, and "rethink their business model".

Once again, luckily, management is usually saved by the very uselessness of the concept for their situation. Most can't come up with a much better plan than making and supplying the products and services they currently provide to the customers they currently serve in more or less the same way they currently operate. They generally confine themselves to announcing organisational changes—playing musical chairs with experienced people who actually know how the business functions. Although this holds back their organisation's progress, at least it doesn't break a working business.

Why, you might ask, would top management in any business call in consultants to advise them if they are already doing OK and then ignore the advice they paid for? We have already explained that most managers have little fundamental understanding of strategy and will go on to show why that situation persists. This limits their confidence in what they are doing and makes them vulnerable to persuasion that they should be doing something else—and senior consultants can be very persuasive! Add to that the journalistic stories in the latest books and journal articles, and we can forgive management for their anxiety. There may be many reasons why the advice does then get acted upon, but a simple inability to do so is common.

There *are* cases where transformation is the only alternative to extinction, but these are extremely rare. The classic case concerns IBM, which faced disaster when its core computer hardware business was decimated by nimbler, lower-cost competitors. In 1993, the company posted what at the time were the largest ever corporate losses of $8 billion. This triggered a deep and fundamental transformation, in which the company shed businesses that were low-margin, required more rapid technology innovation than they could match, and promised too little potential if successful. It focused on the one part of the business where margins and opportunity remained high and competitors were relatively less able to attack: the provision of large and complex corporate IT systems. This is in large part an advisory service, with the sale of hardware and software coming along behind, so the transformation into an IT services specialist was then consolidated by the 2002 acquisition of accountancy firm PwC's consulting business. An impressive story, of course, much written-about and admired—but with *very* few parallels.

Whatever you are doing, change it

A related magic bullet is strategic innovation. This should not be confused with the regular kind of innovation so vital to many businesses. Of course people should constantly be looking out for innovative products and services, or for process innovations ranging from the very small to the quite radical. Toyota, for example, is believed to have implemented over a million changes proposed by the people who actually make its business work. But the more radical the change, the more intensively it should be evaluated and the more carefully it should be implemented, preferably after small-scale tests.

The blizzard of articles, books, and cases on *strategic* innovation has made many companies feel that they should constantly be looking to do fundamentally new things in fundamentally new ways. But this is a huge distraction for managers, who should be spending their time making sure the existing business runs like clockwork, constantly improves, and develops strongly. One large communications corporation started up no fewer than 40 new businesses in a genuinely attractive high-growth sector. But after five years no more than four of these bright ideas had any possibility of being viable, and not one had received more than a small fraction of the money or attention that might have made something worthwhile out of them. The cost? More than a hundred expensive executives working over those five years to show how innovative they could be, but generating no new cash flow and with no prospect of ever doing so.

So widespread is this tendency to follow magic bullets that it can itself become a topic for academic research. Professor Eric Abrahamson of Columbia Business School describes the huge damage done by another related fad that got over-sold and over-bought: "creative destruction."[12] This dangerous notion got promoted on the basis that big, established firms tend not to generate the returns that newly emerging enterprises do[13].

Of course they don't! Most big, high-value firms dominate already developed industries in which most of the potential has largely been captured, along with the growth in profits that can be had from them. The likely stable future cash flows are already factored into their stock price. It's their job to sustain those strong cash flows from their dominant positions, not try to turn themselves into Facebook or Google! Even if

58

we accept that such firms should look for and seize big new opportunities, a dollar invested in them would never reap the same gain as a dollar invested in the pure-play innovators, simply because the gain would be diluted by the stable returns from the core business. And one day, perhaps not so far in the future, Google and Facebook, too, will just be dominant players in mature industries and fail to deliver spectacular returns to shareholders.

Yet the wildest advocates of creative destruction seem to argue that investors would be better off if dowdy old firms like Walmart and Exxon were to throw their core business up in the air and reinvent themselves. The apparent authority behind these exhortations created a stampede amongst executives who thought they were not "with it" unless they were being creatively destructive. As Professor Abrahamson observes, "The 'creative destruction' advocated by change champions has resulted in a painful cycle of initiative overload, change-related chaos, and widespread employee cynicism." Sound familiar?

Two-by-Two Boxes

Along with checklists and bullet points, strategy books and articles are packed with two-by-two grids and other X–Y charts. Such charts mostly claim to work by distinguishing in some way where your company stands compared with others, often with associated performance comparisons, and thus helping you decide where you company *should* be.

An infamous example is the growth-share matrix, developed by the Boston Consulting Group (BCG) in the 1960s[14] and intended to help multi-business corporations decide how to allocate cash (that "allocate" word again) amongst its business units.

Misunderstanding and misuse of this tool led to one of the largest and most disastrous strategy fads of all time: the diversified corporation. Hundreds of companies used the tool during the 1970s to justify buying all kinds of businesses that had nothing in common with each other and running them like an investment portfolio. Cash was allocated or withheld according to the success of each business in relation to how they were supposed to perform, given their position on the grid.

One such company was ITT Corporation, which owned Sheraton Hotels, the Continental Baking Company, Yellow Pages, Hartford Insurance, Avis Rent-a-Car, and a host of other businesses in auto parts, semi-conductors, cosmetics, sewage pumps, for-profit schooling, and other sectors. Most such diversified groups were destroyed during the late 1970s and 1980s by corporate raiders who realised these corporations were actually worth less than the total of the businesses that made them up. Smaller businesses were sold off to more focused companies in their sectors, while larger businesses with strong cash flows were retained. ITT itself only survived this bloodbath by realising in time the danger it was in and dismembering itself before anyone else could do it to them.

Like so many dangerous strategy tools, the growth-share matrix was based on glimmers of useful insight:

- Industries tend to move from high growth rates in their early years to low growth-rates as they mature.

- During the growth phase, companies need to spend a lot of cash to fund R&D, product development, marketing, capacity expansion, and so on.

- As growth slows, competition intensifies, and weaker rivals lose out because they lack the efficiency and market power of larger competitors.

- Eventually, when growth has slowed, only a few large companies survive, but since they have strong sales, good profitability, and little need for any more investment, they generate huge cash flows.

Given this logic, what you want is to move early-growth businesses quickly from low market share to high, where they will be "stars", and invest plenty of cash to build their competitive advantage. Then when growth slows, they become "cash cows", generating strong cash flows that you can invest in more stars. If you don't do this, low-share businesses in early growth become low-share businesses in mature markets, where they become "dogs", failing to generate cash flows due to their weak position. Smaller businesses in fast-growth sectors are therefore "question marks", about which you must make up your mind to either grow them into stars or sell them off. A corporate portfolio, then, can be plotted on the two-by-two chart in Figure 2, the size of each business being reflected in the size of the circles.

It's remarkable how hard it can be to kill off bad ideas. The growth-share matrix approach still featured, as late as 1998, in the upbeat assessment of Tyco's strategy of unrelated diversification. As an article in the Harvard Business Review explained, "Tyco International creates value for its businesses through a set of general management skills and a system of corporate governance."[15] Unlike many other flame-outs of the period, Tyco was not part of the technology bubble but apparently thrived among such unglamorous industries as pipes and valves, fire extinguishers, and diapers. Just a few years after this glowing endorsement from our iconic business journal, Tyco was revealed as yet another case of poor strategic management and financial misreporting.

The diversified conglomerates were not the only companies to err in their use of this tool. Companies with more related businesses also used it to guide their strategy. Otherwise sensible companies, from Shell to Siemens to GE to Disney, jumped on the idea and were tempted to pursue activities they knew nothing about. They noted that the x-axis is relative market share—defined as their own market share divided by that of their largest competitor. This means that only the single largest firm in an industry can lie to the left of 1.0. For example, if you are the market leader and twice as big as number two, your relative share is 2.0, and theirs is 0.5. (The curious feature of the x-axis running from right to left, rather than left to right, is how the matrix was originally shown).

The message seemed crystal clear: only the largest win. So company after company threw huge amounts of cash into becoming number one, by whatever means they could—massive capital investment, acquisitions, price and advertising wars, and so on—destroying profitability in the process and leaving them with no choice but to sell off the "dogs" they created. Why keep throwing money into a losing venture? Because they remained convinced of the ultimate reward and, as is only human nature, were reluctant to admit their error until left with no choice. In boardroom after boardroom, business-unit heads wriggled and squirmed in a desperate attempt to redefine their businesses and their markets in such a way that they would look like "stars" and be rewarded with plenty of cash.

So why are we dwelling on this now ancient history? Because in spite of the 1970s disaster, the growth-share matrix is not dead! BCG themselves have discovered that a large fraction of large global corporations are still using the concept, though most are now doing so in a more intelligent way, to decide on investment and resource priorities. It is to be hoped that less skilful organisations do not rediscover it and recreate the mistakes of 40 years ago.

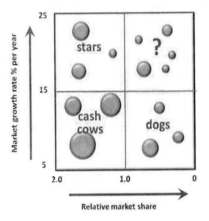

Figure 2: The Growth-Share Matrix

This story illustrates two common and massively important flaws in the logic underpinning many strategy tools.

Describing success does not explain how to become successful.

It may be true that dominant firms in mature markets generate strong cash flows. It may be true that many weaker businesses in fast-growth markets are likely to die. But it doesn't then follow that any less-than-dominant business must become the largest in order to succeed. GM was for decades the largest global auto maker but a cash-burning bonfire, while BMW has never been more than a small fraction of GM's size but highly profitable. In any case, we can't be sure which came first, the chicken or the egg. Were winners profitable because they had the biggest market share, or had they taken the biggest market share by exploiting the cash flows of their superior profitability?

As the GM/BMW comparison illustrates, the growth-share matrix logic becomes especially unreliable when differentiation is possible. Its underlying rationale relies on the principle that as an industry matures, profitability depends on size. But differentiation makes it possible to be very profitable without being the largest competitor, because a substantial fraction of customers are willing to pay more for better products or services.

Comparing winners and losers doesn't work

The second major flaw in the logic of the growth-share matrix is the idea that you can discover answers by grouping stronger and weaker firms and seeing what differs between the two groups. But firms do not fall neatly into winners and losers; performance varies across a spectrum. So some stronger cases will share many features with weaker ones and will differ substantially from other strong ones.

Statistics never lie (?)

This has not stopped a whole industry growing up amongst academics and research organisations desperately searching for causes of superior performance that are allegedly proven by very marginal and dubious statistical differences. To aid in this search, all kinds of ratios have been considered. If a ratio could be dreamed up, someone would try to show it explained something and leap to recommend that management use it.

Tempted? Even today, you can find a version of this wild goose chase in the PIMS service (Profit Impact of Market Strategy) from the Strategic Planning Institute. PIMS proudly promises:

- a database of business strategies used to generate benchmarks and identify winning strategies

- a set of data-derived business strategy principles to guide strategic thinking and strategic measurement

- methodologies for diagnosing business problems and opportunities, and for measuring the profit potential of a business.

Look more closely, however, and it turns out that these bold promises are built on little more than a statistical correlation analysis of piles of data from the institute's subscribing companies. There are hundreds of large, respected corporations on this list, including leaders in major industries, such as GE, Johnson & Johnson, Nestle, Siemens, AT&T and HP. This immense mountain of data apparently shows quite clearly that just 18 variables explain business performance, among them market share, customer concentration, ratio of R&D to sales, operating effectiveness, and capacity utilization. What great news. If you'd like to improve your business performance, all you have to do is get more market share, switch to an industry where there are no large customers, spend more on R&D, get more effective, and increase your capacity utilization. Simple!

The service claims that "years of research on the PIMS database and on other cross-sectional databases of business units show quite clearly that profitability is strongly linked to strategic position. The R square of .65 of a regression of ROI on 18 key strategic variables indicates that strategic positioning is the major determinant of business success."[16] (R square indicates the fraction of variance in the measure of interest that is explained by variances in the causal factors. Zero would mean that none of the variance in ROI is explained and 1.00 would mean that all variance is completely accounted for. This is actually a pretty pathetic level of correlation, and when based on so many variables, is quite meaningless). The next chapter will explain further why correlation studies are, in any case, completely unsuited to seeking explanations for business success.

Benchmarking

This obsession with ratios can be seen in the widespread popularity of benchmarking: comparing a host of metrics about your business with others in your industry. Some research firms even make a living from running anonymous comparison systems whereby businesses in an industry agree to provide data to the survey provider, who then feeds back comparisons between them, concealing the identities of all but the recipient.

Now there can be *some* value in such comparisons when you are sure you are comparing like with like, for example, when looking at yields or quality comparisons between manufacturers of similar products. But it's dangerously misleading to try reading much into benchmarks for more general business measures, especially where firms are far from identical.

One bank I worked with received this kind of comparative data every quarter and spent hours of meeting time poring over each minute difference from its competitors and each deviation since the previous period. It was only when we picked apart the substantive features of the business—its customer profile, product range, marketing mix, channels, service offerings, and so on—that we realized that every single difference existed for very good reasons. The bank was spending more on channel support than most of its competitors, for example, because it was offering a more extensive range of higher-value products. They stopped only just in time; they had been about to cut the very support that justified its premium simply because the benchmarking study had said it was overspending.

A more serious case concerns a benchmarking exercise carried out on the maintenance spending of oil-production companies in the North Sea. A detailed study by a leading consulting firm for one of the major operators concluded that it was grossly overspending on maintenance compared with its most efficient competitors. The firm cut its spending and implemented tight procedures and controls to ensure it did not escalate again. Five years later, the equipment involved was in a dire condition, often breaking down, interrupting production, costing millions of dollars to fix, and even compromising safety. The company had to overspend simply to stop things getting worse. The reality was that this particular firm had been established in the region for longer than its competitors, so its production assets were naturally older than those of more recent arrivals and quite reasonably needed more maintenance.

Resource-based strategy

In the last couple of decades, the strategy field has realised that the kind of crude industry recipes from the 1980s and 1990s have nothing much to offer. Profitability, it turns out, is more a reflection of how well you operate than a result of the industry or sector in which you operate. This is pretty unfortunate given that industry analysis and the hunt for attractive segments still dominate strategy analysis. (The next chapter will show that profitability is the wrong focus for questions of strategy to be asking in any case). Put simply, you can do well in difficult industries, or mess up all on your own even in benign competitive environments.

65

So the next question everyone wanted answered was why some firms in an industry do well while others do poorly.

The immediate answer seemed to be that winners had better resources than losers: more cash, products, people, and so on. But this didn't satisfy the economists, whose credo holds that nothing you can buy, sell, copy, or steal can confer any advantage. No matter if your competitor has more money than you, or twice the number of salespeople; if you have a good business case for the money or the people, the financial markets will provide. The necessary resources will materialize without delay, and without effort on your part.

I once had the following conversation with an economics-based strategy professor in a leading business school (I promise I am not making this up!):

> **Me:** "So you and I operate identical restaurants in the same location, with the same staff, menu, pricing, and customer base. The only difference is that you have $1 million in the bank and I don't—but that is irrelevant?"

> **Professor:** "Correct. You can borrow the same $1 million, and I will bear the opportunity cost of not using my $1 million."

I can't, of course, vouch for whether this professor was representing the purist view correctly, but the gist of the argument is clear enough.

Meanwhile, back in the real world, managers were trying to raise money, hire good staff, develop attractive products, open up strong distribution channels, and build efficient production capacity, all in the apparently misguided belief that these might give them an advantage. Having written off these most tangible of assets as irrelevant, researchers embarked on a hunt for the truly *strategic* resources: those that would confer genuine competitive advantage because your competitors couldn't buy or copy them. They landed on some nicely abstract concepts, such as brand and intellectual capital, and set out to understand the difference between winners and losers in terms of these factors. Unfortunately, they bumped into a familiar problem. Had a firm become a winner because it had these advantages, or had it acquired these advantages by winning?

The evidence was so ephemeral and the conclusions so uncertain that the researchers decided that these inanimate characteristics could not be relied upon to explain success. We needed a still more sophisticated explanation. This duly arrived in the form of "capabilities", plus a later development of the far more exciting-sounding "core competences".

Well, after 20 years of dissecting every cell of this particular cadaver, what are we left with? Endless checklists (again) of the resources and capabilities you should look for, and some more two-by-two boxes. Typically, textbooks suggest that you ask, for each resource or capability, (a) have I got it? and (b) is it important? Figure 3 apparently tells us that the organisation has some strong resources and some weak ones, and that some are strategically important while others are not. What this supposedly tells us is that if you've got something strong and it's important, it's a key strength you should hold on to; if you've got something strong and it isn't important, you're wasting your time with it; if something is important and you haven't got it, you should be worried and go get it; and if it's not important, don't worry about it. Gee, that's helpful!

Frameworks

To add a veneer of respectability, strategy books like to change bullet-point lists into word-and-arrow diagrams called "frameworks". Most of these are simply lists of elements that are claimed to be important, but with no idea how they are specified and no metrics by which to measure them. What they do have is arrows to suggest that the elements are related in some undefined way (and in a way which is usually quite obvious).

Let's see how to create a framework. Here's a list of things that are important to bear in mind to ensure you are successful:

- your objectives
- your approach to achieving them
- your people
- the organisation in which they work
- their capabilities
- the culture among your people
- the procedures you need to make sure everything works.

Reasonable principles to be sure, but such a list is simply not special enough to be considered a major breakthrough idea in strategy. So let's sprinkle some magic dust over the list and see what we can do with it.

Well, objectives are like *goals*, your approach is your *strategy*, your people are *staff*, and the way they are organized is their *structure*. Capabilities are *skills*, we can think of culture as the *style* in which your organisation operates, and procedures are *systems*. Hey, all but one of these begin with "s"! Hmm, what can we do with "goals"? Let's add an adjective and call them *"superordinate goals"*. No-one ever uses the word superordinate, but what the heck? It sounds important, and that way each item begins with "s".

So there we have it: the 7S list of things to think about in order to be successful: superordinate goals, strategy, staff, structure, skills, style, and systems.

Wait a minute, though. This is just another list; can't we make it into one of those powerful framework things? Sure! Arrange the items in a diagram and connect them up with arrows! (Figure 4).

OK, so it's a pretty good idea to have the right people with the right skills and the right attitude using the right approaches and

Figure 3: Assessing resources and capabilities

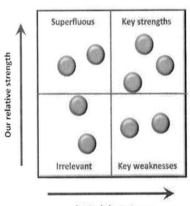

being organized in the right way. But what exactly is management to do with this framework? All we find in the many books and articles that explain the idea is a few anecdotes giving examples of organisations where the 7 Ss are in good shape and doing well or in bad shape and doing badly. Like just about all strategy frameworks, it fails on all of the requirements for a reliable professional tool; it provides no clear specification of the terms or means of measuring them, no proven causality between them, no link at all to any performance outcome we are trying to achieve, and no cumulative evidence for how exactly it works or what it achieves.

What causes what?

Not all frameworks are fancy ways of presenting a list of the blindingly obvious. Some genuinely try to show causality, which should in principle be helpful. If we know what causes what, then we can see how management decisions can change the causal factors so as to improve the outcomes.

Figure 5, for example, is typical of many diagrams that appear early on in strategy textbooks in an effort to show how the whole field fits together. It appears to say that:

- Resources create Capabilities.

- Capabilities compared with industry Success Factors determine your Competitive Advantage.

- Your Competitive Advantage determines your Performance.

Such charts reflect the consensus of dozens of theoretical papers written over many decades and are broadly accepted by experienced academics who specialize in understanding such things. They try to distil something useful from academic debates, but they create several problems for any executive with the time and patience to try using them.

First, yet again, the words are abstract and vague. We already explained that the field can't even define Competitive Advantage or Performance, and this fluff continues: what exactly is a Resource and how is it different from a Capability? The textbooks and articles upon which this framework is based give any number of definitions, but the explanations use even more abstract words, multiplying the confusion. Faced with such language, teams can spend hours arguing over semantics without ever being much the wiser.

Secondly, even if we agree on definitions, we hit another problem: it isn't clear how to *measure* what we are talking about. The books give case examples to shed light on the terms used in their frameworks and to show how they are supposed to work, but these cases are so brief and lacking in solid fact that they provide no real insight at all. It turns out that the very research upon which such frameworks are based is equally vague about the real measures. Since researchers can't define and measure an actual Capability, for example, they rely on proxies instead. If you don't have a measure for, say, the product development capability of firms in a study, why not take the product range itself as an indicator?

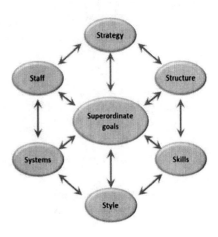

Lacking any sound definition of terms or explicit measure for them, the framework falls apart completely. The arrows linking the words are supposed to imply that if you know what item A is, you can calculate or estimate item B. But if you don't know how to define A and haven't got a measure for it, how are you supposed to determine B? Capabilities are supposed to cause Competitive Advantage, which in turn is supposed to cause Performance. But the only one of these items we might actually have a number for is performance, probably measured by profitability, so we can't in practice put together any kind of analysis to explain actual numbers in real cases. We certainly can't put any concrete estimate on what might happen to profitability if we were to have X percent more of any particular Capability. Indeed, we don't know how to measure the Capability we already have, so we can't possibly know what X percent more would look like.

Once again, this framework fails on all the requirements for being a useful and reliable professional tool.

Explain everything!

Perhaps the best-known and widely used framework is the balanced scorecard from Kaplan and Norton[18]. Strictly, this is not, and doesn't claim to be, a tool for *developing* strategy; rather, it is concerned with *controlling* strategy. It is certainly an improvement over purely financial controls, bringing in issues from three other domains: the customer's perspective, internal processes, and the organisation's pursuit of learning and growth. It also provides a structured approach for making sure that the logic of strategic initiatives makes sense. But it can be dangerous if, as is easily done, it is wrongly applied.

Take one real company's strategic initiative to improve its sales process so as to drive growth ahead of the market. Its balanced scorecard

Figure 5: How resources and capabilities drive performance

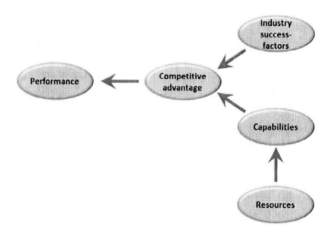

approach took it through the following logic, reflecting the four themes outlined by Kaplan and Norton:

- Apply your marketing skills, and use your customer information . . .

- …to respond to customers faster than competitors . . .

- … improving value for money and strengthening customer relationships…

- … and thus drive sales, margin, and profitability.

The only problem was that though customers were indeed thrilled at the quick response to their enquiries, the company didn't have the capacity to fulfil the demand that this improvement created. Customer relationships were actually *damaged* by this initiative, sales were *lost* rather than gained, and profits fell.

Important interdependencies such as these are often simply missed — a common problem that makes balanced scorecards, as well as their offspring, strategy maps[19], not up to the job of steering strategy. Indeed, the connections implied in most such scorecards and strategy maps are little more than a plausible selection of just a few of the factors that might be involved. But perhaps the most astounding omissions in many organisations' balanced scorecards is that they include no information whatsoever on the market or on the activities of competitors. Changes in these two domains can't possibly be irrelevant to your best choice of strategy and its effective implementation.

Another drawback of balanced scorecards is that they cannot handle how things change over time. Winning new customers may be a priority today, but next year it may no longer be feasible (perhaps all the available

customers have been captured), and the new priority should be building average sales to each customer. The cell phone industry provides a good example: once everyone was using the service, companies needed to shift attention from capturing customers to increasing their usage and spending.

Sorry he can't come out to fight
he's watching a ball game...

Scorecards also suffer from one of the key weaknesses of simpler strategy tools: they feature concepts that are too abstract and ambiguous to be meaningfully measurable, such as customer communication, effective guidelines, and management learning. This opens the door to low-grade consultants and trainers offering advice and courses on how to develop and use these tools. One senior executive complained to me furiously about a one-day training event in which tutors were supposed to help participants learn how to use the balanced scorecard, yet there were just four tutors for more than 100 participants. The event was billed as being led by Professor Kaplan, but his only appearance was via a short video link; although doubtless he was unaware of the misrepresentation. Events like this give a bad name to those who genuinely try to offer professional advice on scorecards and other respectable tools, and destroy any value executives might otherwise be able to extract.

So we see the same problems with balanced scorecards as with other strategy tools: abstract and ambiguous terminology, no demonstrable casual relationships, and no replicability. The content and quality of what you get is heavily dependent on who happens to do the work.

A useful few

It is important in this attack on the poor methods and tools in strategy not to throw out the baby with the bath water. Some have a degree of underlying rigour; some are a little useful in some cases; some, as we have seen, can be useful, but also potentially dangerous if misused.

The Experience Curve

Developed by the Boston Consulting Group in the 1960s, this method explains how unit costs of novel manufactured products fall as a company's cumulative production (its "experience") grows.[20] In industries as diverse as computer hard drives, aircraft production, and wind power, unit costs fall by a characteristic percentage each time the total amount of output ever produced doubles. So, for example, it may cost 20 percent less to produce the 100th aircraft of a type than the 50th, and 20 percent less again to produce the 200th. A critical result of this is that as the industry grows, it takes longer and longer for each doubling of cumulative output to happen, and so unit costs fall more slowly over time.

This reduction in unit cost as output increases does not happen automatically, of course; manufacturers have to work at it. But if you are such a company, understanding the rate at which unit cost decreases is very helpful. It tells you, for example, how fast you will likely need to drive down costs in order to stay competitive. It also tells you when the cost of your technology might reach the point at which it can compete with existing alternatives. We can have a reasonable idea, for example, how long it will take before solar cells are cheap enough to substitute for other energy sources in various applications.[21]

An important reason that the experience curve is so useful is that it is one of the very few strategy tools that help explain how things change over time. This means it is constantly giving you new information, allowing you to continually update your expectations and plans.

The "Five Forces"

The Five Forces method for assessing the impact of competition and other factors on the profitability of an industry is probably the most widely known of the serious strategy tools. It essentially says that profits get competed away over time, at a rate that depends not just on how many competitors there are, but also on the risk of new competitors entering the industry, the ability of customers to switch between those competitors, the power of any providers of important and scarce inputs to demand high prices, and the availability of substitutes.[22]

Although difficult to apply with much confident quantification, the method nevertheless can give an indication of how average industry profitability might change, and the scope that may exist to do somewhat better (or worse!) than that average. It also offers clues as to how to position the business to stand a chance of getting to that higher-profit position.

Being now some 30 years old, it is only to be expected that the faddishness of strategy leads many self-appointed experts to dismiss the method as irrelevant to today's complex, fast-moving, and hyper-competitive world. But the fact is that there is a perfectly sound five-forces story to tell about the emergence of industries as diverse as low-fare airlines, cell phones, flat-screen TVs, and even web browsers and social networks, to a degree.

The Value Curve

This method illustrates how customers balance or value different benefits provided by alternative products or services. To illustrate the point, Figure 6 is a "value curve analysis" for a low-fare airline, such as Southwest, compared with normal, full-service airlines. Low-fare services offer very low prices to customers, in exchange for not offering many benefits of full-service airlines. (Many different versions of this chart appear in various books and articles, reflecting the somewhat approximate assessment of the factors involved, but all offer similar insights.)

74

The story is not quite so simple, however, because the resulting high passenger volumes of low-fare airlines mean that they can typically offer many more destinations within a given region. And in Europe's congested air space, the use of secondary airports means that some low-fare airlines can actually be more punctual, not less. Certain airlines also choose intriguing and important variations on the basic low-fare model. easyJet, for example, makes a particular virtue of flying to major airports and even offers business-style departure lounges to anyone willing to pay.

What mix of benefits to offer to customers, as Figure 6 illustrates, is a key part of the strategic positioning choice. The Value Curve is therefore somewhat useful, but its basic insight does not change much over time: using this analysis, you would have got pretty much the same answer when Southwest was started over 30 years ago as you would today. But many companies use a related, though more sophisticated, tool from Marketing—conjoint analysis—to make detailed and continually updated choices about their products and services.[23]

Figure 6: Value Curve assessment of low-fare airlines, compared with others

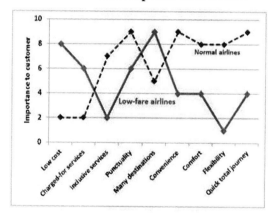

The table, following, indicates the value of some common strategy tools, though it is not intended to be an exhaustive list. It also assesses the potential value of the tools for public-sector, voluntary, and other non-corporate organisations. (This is generally low, since strategy's foundations lie in research concerning profit-making companies.) The table also indicates the effort required for a method to deliver any real value, that is, data-gathering, analysis, and interpretation. Finally, it assesses the degree of danger resulting from misuse of the method.

The table includes some items that we have not discussed in this chapter, simply for reasons of space. See www.12manage.com for a more extensive list of tools, methods, and frameworks, together with summary explanations. Beware, though, that most are of little or no value, for reasons explained in this chapter.

The table does not include methods that rely on abstract or subjective language, and even those that are included will be devalued if this is how they are used. The exception is scenario planning, which can be valuable, even if used descriptively.

	Value for positioning	Value for continuing management	Usefulness for non-commercial cases	Effort needed for competent work	Danger if misused
Industry forces ("5 forces")	*****	**	*	****	*
Industry Segmentation	*****	***	*	****	*
Value chain	*****	****	**	***	*
Value curve	*****	****	**	***	*
Value-based management	****	***	**	****	*****
Scenario planning	****	****	*	*****	****
Experience curve	****	**	**	**	**
Balanced scorecard	****	***	**	****	***
Growth-share matrix	*****	**	*	*	****

TIPS

What does all this add up to? A load of bullet-point lists, two-by-two boxes, and abstract frameworks, few of which are actually used by anyone. If they are used, they offer little or no value and can cause more trouble than if management were to have nothing at all. So how can you avoid these dangers and squeeze just a little bit of value from the strategy tools and methods out there?

- First, set appropriately low expectations for what you and your team will likely get from any strategy work you decide to do—so you can at least reduce the cynicism that will result when big expectations are disappointed.

- Check out the tools that have some likely value for assessing the strength of your business's strategic position. Read the original, authoritative source, and investigate the case examples thoroughly.

- If the tools you investigate suggest that there may be some weakness or potential for strengthening your strategic position, study the methods carefully, work out which one (or more) you will use, and exactly how you are going to do it.

- If the result of this work suggests a quite radical change to what you are currently doing (which is very unlikely in most cases), you will need to think carefully about whether you can do it. Unfortunately, there are no tools to help you do that.

- Consider whether adopting some version of the balanced scorecard might help you steer your strategy and performance—but don't forget to add regular checks on what is happening, or could happen, to your market, and what competitors might do.

- Each business situation is unique, so a generalized one-size-fits-all approach will likely not provide the answers you're looking for.

- If you are in a non-business situation—sorry!

Notes

1. See, for example, Richard Rumelt, 2011, Good Strategy Bad Strategy: The Difference and Why It Matters, New York: Crown Business.

2. Robert S. Kaplan and David P. Norton, 2001, The Strategy-Focused Organization: How Balanced Scorecard Companies Thrive in the New Business Environment, Boston: Harvard Business School Press.

3. Darrell Rigby and Barbara Bilodeau, 2011, Management Tools and Trends, 2011, Bain & Company. Retrieved 28-3-12.

4. To understand professional scenario-based planning, see the articles by members of Royal Dutch Shell's strategy team that brought it to widespread attention in the 1980s, including: Pierre Wack, 1985, "Scenarios: Uncharted Waters Ahead", Harvard Business Review, 63(5), pp. 73–89; Pierre Wack, 1985, "Scenarios: Shooting the Rapids", Harvard Business Review, 63(6), pp. 139–150; and Arie de Geus, 1988, "Planning as Learning", Harvard Business Review, 66(2), pp. 70–74.

5. Michael Porter, 1980, Competitive Strategy: Techniques for Analyzing Industries and Competitors, New York: The Free Press; Michael Porter, 1985, Competitive Advantage: Creating and Sustaining Superior Performance, New York: The Free Press.

6. Renée Dye and Olivier Sibony, 2007, "How to Improve Strategic Planning", McKinsey Quarterly, August, pp. 40–49. Retrieved 28-3-2012.

7. George Stalker, Jr. and Robert Lachenauer, 2004, "Hardball: Five Killer Strategies for Trouncing the Competition", Harvard Business Review, 82, pp. 62–71.

8. Michael Treacy and Fred Wiersema, 1997, The Discipline of Market Leaders: Choose Your Customers, Narrow Your Focus, Dominate Your Market, New York: Basic Books.

9. See, for example, Monica Franco, Robert Wiseman, Bernadine Johnson Dykes, and Roman Weidlich, 2011, "Pursuing a Dual Strategy of Exploitation and Exploration", Think: Cranfield. Retrieved 20-3-2012.

10. A good tool for this kind of investigation is Google Scholar, a search system designed specifically for tracking down academic articles and related books.

11. This thesis can be found at http://www.reocities.com/WallStreet/exchange/4280/.

12. Eric Abrahamson, 2004, Change Without Pain: How Managers Can Overcome Initiative Overload, Organizational Chaos, and Employee Burnout, Boston: Harvard Business School Press.

13. Richard Foster and Sarah Kaplan, 2001, Creative Destruction: Why Companies that Are Built to Last Underperform the Market—and How to Successfully Transform Them, New York: Doubleday.

14. Bruce Henderson, 1973, "The Experience Curve—Reviewed (Part IV): The Growth Share Matrix or The Product Portfolio", BCG Perspectives, 175, Boston Consulting Group. Carl Stern and Michael Deimler, 2006, The Boston Consulting Group on Strategy: Classic Concepts and New Perspectives, Hoboken, NJ: John Wiley & Sons,

Inc., pp. 12–39.

15. David Collis and Cynthia Montgomery, 1998, "Creating Corporate Advantage", Harvard Business Review, May–June, pp. 71–83.

16. http://pimsonline.com/about_pims_db.htm. Retrieved 24-4-2012.

17. R. H. Waterman, T. J. Peters, and J. R. Phillips, 1980, "Structure Is Not Organisation", Business Horizons, 23(3), June, pp. 14–26.

18. Robert S. Kaplan and David P. Norton, 1996, The Balanced Scorecard: Translating Strategy into Action, Boston: Harvard Business School Press.

19. Strategy maps go beyond just measuring and reporting the four domains of performance covered by balanced scorecards. They enable management to lay out a logical time-phased series of initiatives to be taken in each of these domains so as to improve strategy and performance. See Robert S. Kaplan and David P. Norton, 2004, Strategy Maps: Converting Intangible Assets into Tangible Outcomes, Boston: Harvard Business School Press.

20. Bruce Henderson, 1973, "The Experience Curve Reviewed", in Carl Stern and Michael S. Deimler, Eds., 2006, The Boston Consulting Group on Strategy: Classic Concepts and New Perspectives, Hoboken: John Wiley & Sons, Inc., pp. 12–24, gives a number of examples.

21. Patrick Hearps and Dylan McConnell, 2011, Renewable Energy Technology Cost Review, Melbourne Energy Institute. Retrieved 8-4-2012.

22. Michael Porter, 1980, Competitive Strategy: Techniques for Analyzing Industries and Competitors, New York: TheFree Press; Michael Porter, 1985, Competitive Advantage: Creating and Sustaining Superior Performance, New York: The Free Press.

23. See, for example, Ronald Wilcox, 2011, A Practical Guide to Conjoint Analysis. Kindle Edition.

CHAPTER FOUR

WHY THE TOOLS DON'T WORK

"Your theories are the worst kind of popular tripe, your methods are sloppy, and your conclusions are highly questionable. You are a poor scientist, Dr Venkman!"

Dean Yeager in Ghostbusters, 1984

It's pretty easy to spot some basic problems with the so-called science claimed to lie behind the strategy tools on offer. So maybe the fact that few executives use strategy tools suggests that they are quite smart. They may not be able to put their finger on exactly *why* they are sceptical; they just don't have any faith in the tools. This chapter looks at some of the problems in the foundations that supposedly support these tools to see whether the way they are developed may be at fault.

Others, too, are both puzzled and frustrated by the mess that strategy is in. In 2000, strategy consultants McKinsey & Company concluded a two-year study entitled the **Strategy Theory Initiative**. This was a fundamental and thorough review of all the academic literature in the field, along with all the consultants' tools they could find, and was intended to identify the really powerful theories and methods. After two years of work by a team of some of their brightest and most experienced consultants, they found virtually nothing.

Sure, there was the microeconomics that seemed to help explain how profitability might look in different situations, but it told management little about what to actually do. Then there was game theory, which might help with some particular types of decision making in rather idiosyncratic circumstances but wasn't of much general use.

There was also a bunch of things to do with financial analysis and control: value-chain analysis (a souped-up way of looking at cost ratios and margins), plus value-based management, and the balanced scorecard from Kaplan and Norton. These kind of work for keeping things under control but don't tell you much of any use about strategy: the vital questions of what to do, when, and how much in order to bring about what likely level of sustained growth in healthy performance.

The study found some topics that were widely discussed in academic literature, such as evolutionary theory and the resource-based approach, but seemed to be of little or no value for tackling the strategic challenges facing real organisations. Other than that, there were a few methods that sounded OK but seemed to work only in the hands of the people who devised them and a few devoted followers, such as core competences and soft-systems methodology (a way of describing the various interacting relationships in a business system).

The study concluded that strategy is important but that there are few useful methods on offer for doing it.

Of ivory towers and the usual suspects

Now you might expect the strategy academics to be concerned that the great ideas they took a lifetime to develop are of no use to anyone in the real world. But until recently, they seemed not to be at all! For example, after years of effort on the strategy process (how strategy gets developed and implemented, as opposed to what that strategy is or should be), even top academics who worked on this stuff recognized that no-one in management actually used it.[1] But that hasn't stopped plenty of others carrying on regardless. It is still a top research topic to this day.

Others labour under the misapprehension that their tools are used. And the evidence for their self-confidence? The tools must be used because they feature in textbooks, management journals, and business school courses. Take this comment from an article in an academic strategy journal: "Resource-based view logic is nearly ubiquitous as a <u>practical</u>

tool [original emphasis] as evidenced by its coverage in strategy classes, textbooks, and journals with largely managerial audiences."[2]

In fact, the resource-based view is only a favourite way of thinking about strategy among academics. Perhaps the authors might drop into a management conference and carry out some grounded research there. They could first ask the audience to name any strategy approaches they have heard of, then offer them a list of twenty or so approaches and see how many of them tick "resource-based view". The approach features in classes, textbooks, and journals only because academics produce them, not because anyone uses them!

One research study claimed to discover that strategy methods *are* widely used, and offered a toolbox of the most common and useful methods.[3] On closer inspection, though, we find that the survey was carried out only amongst graduates of top business schools. This is like carrying out a survey in maternity clinics and concluding that every woman in the country is pregnant and taking vitamins! It is also likely that the responses were heavily skewed, people who do not use the methods probably not responding to the survey in the first place.

In the absence of much solid wisdom from the academics, pioneering corporations and consulting firms have come up with methods of their own. We already saw that the Boston Consulting Group originated the experience curve and the growth-share matrix. And it was largely Royal Dutch Shell that developed scenario-based planning into a usable method. Unfortunately, these are rare examples of high-quality concepts which—if not misunderstood and misused—can be useful. Regrettably, others with far weaker foundations get taken up simply because they are well marketed.

Valuable nuggets

One of the frustrating features of the chaos that passes as a professional toolkit for strategy is that underneath all the mysticism and fog, there is often a trace of something valid. Take the famous Five Forces framework from Michael Porter, discussed at the end of Chapter 3. It's true that customers are powerful when they are few in number and large in size. It's true that few new firms enter a market when big barriers have to be overcome. It's true that profitability will be competed away when there are too many competitors. The trouble is that there are so many other things going on that we can hardly ever extract any useful numbers from these broad principles.

Because strategy concepts are so ambiguous and ill-defined, their failure when management tries to apply them is not because they are fundamentally wrong, but because they have been misrepresented, misunderstood, or misapplied — or all three. The principle of core competences, for example, has been used by many organisations not so much to focus on critical sources of advantage as to neglect other factors that are important.

Take Honda for example. In 1990, the company was in trouble. As the *Economist* reported at the time "… [the company] was in thrall to its engineers — a priesthood…untroubled by the dismal business of marketing and accounting…It hardly seemed to matter that customers were not buying Honda's flights of engineering fancy…Things were already going wrong [due to lack of] attention to what the customer wanted and producing it at reasonable cost…It was taking twice as long to get a new Honda into production as Toyota." Yet 1990 was also the year that Honda was cited as a great example of the core competences principle, deemed to have a huge competitive advantage because of its powerful core competence in four-stroke engines.[4]

We see this again and again: a concept or approach to strategy has a glimmer of something that may be useful, in some cases, at some times, but it gets distorted and magnified into something dangerous and inappropriate.

Right phenomenon: wrong explanation

Consider the concept of the "tipping point"[5]. Correctly identified and carefully documented at the outset, it was badly misrepresented and subsequently misapplied. The basic idea behind the tipping point is that relatively small differences can give rise to the rapid escalation of important changes, such as the growth in popularity of a new product.

However, people leapt on the idea that the process at work here is a form of self-reinforcing growth, rather like an infection: the more people have something, the more new people get it. So, for example, a few early adopters buy the iPad and like it, they tell their friends, and the purchase rate skyrockets. Now this mechanism does occur and can be very powerful, but rapid growth is not strictly a tipping point. If sales of a

84

product in successive months are 10,000, 40,000, 100,000, 200,000, and 350,000, for example, the growth rate is actually *slowing*, not accelerating.

Many tipping-point cases reflect a quite different mechanism: the crossing of a threshold. The rapid growth of the cell phone industry in China during the 1990s may well look like a word-of-mouth process, but that's only part of the story. Hundreds of millions of Chinese people at the time knew what a cell phone was and why it might be useful, and would have liked to buy one, but simply could not afford it. But there is an income threshold where a cell phone *does* become affordable, and rapid economic growth pushed a fraction of those millions over the threshold each month. As long as most people remained well below the income threshold, growth was slow; at the point where average disposable income came close to the threshold, growth was phenomenal; and once incomes reach the level where most people are well above the threshold, everyone who wants a cell phone will have one, at which point first-time purchases will dry up.

There was indeed a tipping point at which the Chinese cell phone market took off, but that tipping point occurred when the falling costs of ownership crossed consumers' income threshold. As it happens, cell phones have not been the only market showing extraordinary growth in China; life insurance is also skyrocketing, though it's hardly a market driven by word of mouth among excited new customers!

Changes in price and functionality also cause tipping points. Take hydrogen-fuelled cars. Sure, a handful of early adopters will buy the things, even when they don't work well and are ridiculously expensive. But the infection mechanism won't trigger anything much if that's where things stay. Functionality and price will each have to pass a threshold of acceptability before the mass market feels they are worthwhile and affordable — and *then* we will see the tipping point.

Does it matter that a phenomenon is identified correctly but is given an explanation that is grossly inaccurate? Absolutely! If you think your market would take off if only you could find those early adopters and get them spreading the word, you will devote your efforts to target marketing. But if the truth is that the product is not good enough or affordable enough, you will still be scratching you head years later, wondering why that tipping point thing never happened. If you think your market is driven by reaching a threshold of functionality, you will focus on product improvements, and if you think it's driven by affordability, you will focus on cost reduction. But if the truth is that not enough people know about the product in order to try it and tell others about it, you will fail again, but for quite different reasons.

Reader, beware!

When you read an article or book about some idea in strategy or management, watch out for two contrasting approaches.

The first style is descriptive, telling you what the writer has seen or discovered through observation and investigation. This kind of research and writing rests on the justification that it is futile trying to find out why anything is as it is, so the best we can do is simply describe what there is.

The second style is prescriptive, telling you how best something should be done. In these cases, the authors go further and imply that they have looked at success and failure and can therefore explain how the circumstances differ between the two and confidently advise you on the best choices to make.

But beware: it is often unclear which of the two approaches is being followed. Articles that describe how things are done frequently imply that this is the way they should best be done. Much of what has been written about emergent or "crafting" approaches to strategy, for example, falls into this category. This is exceedingly dangerous because it can mislead you into thinking, "Ah, if Famous Corp. does strategy like this, it must be good, so I'd best do the same."

Prescriptive articles can be equally dangerous. Unless the approach being promoted has been tested in a wide range of situations, you can't be sure it will be right for you or your particular circumstances. A responsible article in this style will tell you not only what it recommends you to do but also the possible limitations or exceptions where the approach doesn't—or may not—work.

So we can question what the strategy academics have offered on two grounds:

1. If the academics were doing their job properly, there would

be no place for the kind of feeble and dangerous approaches that come from the worst consultants and from writers who have never done any real strategy work in their lives.

2. If academics' output was built on solid foundations, it would be clear when consultants or executives misrepresent or misuse the resulting strategy methods. Like the engineers who turn the science of aerodynamics into the engineering of safe, high-performance aircraft, strategy professionals should be able to rely on sound science from the academics to develop powerful approaches to strategic management—but they can't.

So how come all the seemingly clever stuff on strategy is either useless or dangerous, or—as we have seen—misrepresented or misused? What should happen is that research is conducted to identify why things happen as they do, and academics then test and validate the policies and decisions that management can implement to improve things in the real world.

Perhaps we're asking the wrong question?

Since the purpose of business strategy is to help a company make money, natural questions to ask are "What drives the level of profitability in an industry?" (so we can choose which industry or segment to focus on) and "How can we become more profitable?" And these questions do indeed seem to dominate strategy research.

Various measures may be looked at, depending on what exactly the researcher is trying to do and what data is actually available: return on sales, return on invested capital, return on equity, the ratio between economic value added and capital employed, and so on. Industries show marked differences on these measures, so it would seem useful to find out which do best. You will find a table of industry profitability rankings in many of the strategy textbooks.[6] Pharmaceuticals, medical equipment, tobacco, and computer software come out quite well, for example, while building materials, railroads, airlines, and petrochemicals seem to do poorly.

Well, that's easy, then—get out of petrochemicals and into drugs. No one makes *quite* such naïve suggestions, of course; people realise that you need the right resources and capabilities to operate in an industry, and you can't simply transplant those you have into an activity you know nothing about. But perhaps we can extend this approach to look inside an industry and find some segments that are more profitable than others: low-fare airlines as opposed to full-service airlines, say. We could also look to see if there are systematic differences between what more profitable and less profitable firms do.

And this, in essence, is what the vast majority of strategy research does. Studies start from a hypothesis that some features of an industry or firm produce superior profitability and a plausible rationale by which this might be true. They then collect data on these features and deploy statistical analysis to see whether these features are indeed correlated with profitability.

What could possibly be wrong with that? Surely we all want to be more profitable. Figure 7 below shows how different competitors in an industry might differ in profitability. We have a couple of small, unprofitable competitors, a few moderately profitable competitors, some quite large, and just one most-profitable company. We might want to be the "best position" company, making above-average profits and being large enough for those profits to be significant. So if we can find a persuasive explanation for why some firms are more profitable than others, we can copy what they do and—ta-da!—our profitability will increase.

Unfortunately, we have known since 1959 that superior profitability is neither sustainable nor particularly interesting: it isn't what investors value, nor is it (or should it be) the dominant focus of what management seeks to do.[7] How so? Simple. If you had $100 to invest, would you rather get back $12 a year for ever, or $5 this year, $10 next year, then $15, $25, $40 . . .? It's earnings growth that investors value, not percentage margins.

Strictly speaking, the value of a business or an initiative undertaken by a business is the present value of future free cash flows. In simple terms, "free cash flow" is operating cash flow minus any cash reinvested—in other words, what is left over to distribute to investors. If you aren't familiar with this basic principle, which has been axiomatic in the Finance field for half a century, you should be! It is well established and clearly laid out in authoritative sources.[8] If you want to see how well one leading company CEO understands the point, take a look at the letter from Jeff Bezos, head of Amazon.com, which opens the company's 2007 Annual Report.[9]

It is depressing how poorly some executives understand this principle and its implications.[10] The board of one listed company stated in bold at the beginning of its strategic plan that it intended to "constantly exceed stockholder expectations." Just think what this implies. Investors value what they expect future cash flow to be—*including growth*. If this firm makes $100 million one year and $120 million the next, stockholders will reckon the firm is growing at 20 percent a year, and unless told otherwise are likely to expect $144 million the next. So simply making more money each year is not enough; investors *already* expect it, and the stock price will reflect it. To constantly exceed investors' expectations, this firm must deliver an *ever-faster* growth rate in earnings.

Figure 7: The spread of profitability in an industry

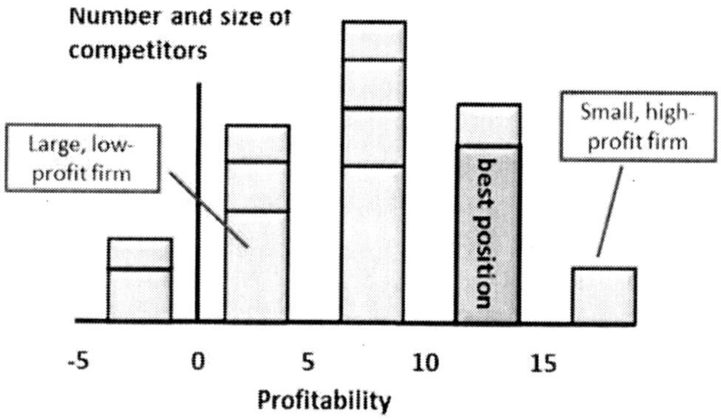

There is a further reason to look at growth of free cash flow as the main indicator of good strategic management: the differences in performance on this measure are truly massive! The superior performance of Southwest Airlines and Ryanair as far as investors are concerned is not a few percentage points of extra return on invested capital (ROIC), though both do well on that measure. It is because both have created cash flows out of sight of their weaker competitors. Amazon.com was never superior to other online retailers because it delivered higher ROIC either, but because it too grew revenue and cash flow out of sight of any competitor. The same is true of pretty much all the poster children of strategic success that we all love to talk about and want to emulate.

Performance differences measured by cash flow growth are orders-of-magnitude greater than differences in profitability measures.

Fortunately, investors are not quite so unrealistic and recognize that firms can't keep this near-exponential growth up for ever in real life. Even firms like Google—or, in their day, Microsoft—must reach limits to their potential, so growth rates are bound to slow at some point. This makes it as important for executives to manage investors' expectations (tell them what to expect and why) as it is to manage actual earnings.

Even otherwise smart commentators seem to misunderstand the point about earnings, growth, and value. Right from the beginning of *Good to Great*, much is made of the fact that the good to great companies delivered much higher returns than supposed icons of corporate America such as GE.[11] But of course they did. GE's accomplishments have put it right at the top of major industries, so that neither these industries nor GE itself have the headroom for spectacular growth. The companies were deliberately chosen for the book on the basis that they had changed from unspectacular players in their industries into high-growth stars— which is possible only for a firm that is a minor contender in the first place. None of this negates the value of the book's main purpose and findings, but it does show how easy it is to draw meaningless conclusions from comparisons of earnings growth and shareholder returns.

Another book that falls into the same trap is *Creative Destruction* (a notion introduced in the last chapter), which berates companies like GE, DuPont, and Exxon for failing to deliver spectacular growth rates, and criticizes the "cultural lock-in" that prevents them from reinventing themselves.[12] It points out that "the US economy is dominated by companies that were not large enough to qualify in the top 80 percent in 1962."

What exactly were we supposed to see instead? Exxon becoming the leader in PC software, DuPont the largest supermarket retailer, or Coca-Cola the top social networking business? Of course these firms haven't matched the growth rates of powerful players in emerging industries. How could they? Microsoft, Walmart, Google, and the rest of today's superstars will in turn fail to maintain spectacular percentage growth rates in future years. No one seriously expects otherwise, and their management will not have failed by merely sustaining strong earnings.

90

Fortunately, not all executives are cowed by this kind of beating. When he took over as McDonald's chairman and chief executive officer in 2002, Jim Cantalupo told investors:

> "We have struggled to grow our business in the face of weak and uncertain economic conditions around the world. The result has been disappointing financial performance. This is not acceptable. It didn't take me long to realize that some difficult—albeit necessary—decisions had to be made.
>
> To start, we are **targeting a lower earnings growth** rate [emphasis added]. Given the nature and size of our business, the prior earnings-per-share growth target in the 10- to 15-percent range is no longer realistic. Yet, we are committed to returning the company to reliable, sustainable annual sales and earnings-per-share growth. We also have decided to lower our capital expenditures compared with recent years until we achieve significant improvements in sales, margins, and returns at our 30,000 existing McDonald's restaurants. We will concentrate our capital spending on those investments with the greatest potential. This strategic allocation of capital will free up a significant amount of cash, which we intend to use to strengthen our financial position and improve returns to shareholders.
>
> In short, McDonald's is in transition from a company that emphasizes 'adding restaurants to customers' to one that emphasizes 'adding customers to restaurants.'" [13]

This is a mature company in a mature industry, and its leadership responsibility is a strategy that sustains strong earnings, not one that pursues unrealistic growth or unsustainable profitability. Even when growth opportunities are finished and we are trying to cope with maturity or decline, percentage profitability is a foolish focus. In extreme cases, investors are not only content but keen to invest in loss-making businesses for many years, in the knowledge that these businesses are building the potential for strong earnings in the future.

Amazon delivered impressive losses from 1996 through 2001, hitting its lowest point with an operating loss of $863 million in 2000. Yet investors were eager to support the company over this prolonged period of cash burn because they were confident it was building a platform for strong future cash flows. Even if they didn't expect to keep hold of their stock until the day these positive results materialized, someone else would share their confidence and be prepared to buy their stock at a good price.

So what would our research have found if we had been looking to explain profitability in a sample of businesses including Amazon? We would have been trying to understand why other firms were profitable while Amazon was not, with a view to doing what the profitable firms were doing and avoiding what Amazon was up to!

Strategy is *for the future*

This kind of thing perplexes real-world executives. I talked to one CEO who had taken part in a research study investigating whether it was preferable for firms to expand internationally or focus on the home market. As usual, the researcher had promised to share his findings with the participating organisations and duly did so. He explained to the CEO that the results were unexpectedly discouraging. Although they had expected to find that international expansion was advantageous, it actually seemed to damage profitability.

The CEO shared his puzzlement with me. He had taken part in the research because he genuinely wanted to understand the benefits of international expansion in his industry, but he didn't understand why the research had focused on profitability: "I could have told him at the start that our profitability would be held back by going into new markets. We have to set up sales operations and market our products to customers who have never heard of us. Of course it's going to cost us, perhaps for many years, before we get significant profits coming back. Am I going to go on with it? You bet!"

To be fair, some research recognizes this problem and tries to adjust for it, for example, by looking at the relationship between *today's* profitability and suspected causal factors in previous years. Perhaps profitability in the industry we just discussed would be correlated with international expansion several years earlier? But then we get into a whole lot of other difficulties. How long a delay should we consider? How do we allow for the fact that particular decisions or activities rarely continue for many years?

Even when different firms follow similar strategies, they will likely do so at different times and at different rates, so no particular pair of dates will capture the same phenomenon across most firms. And on top of these difficulties, a thousand other things will be happening, each with its own particular delays, each interfering with the rest, and all likely to affect the profitability number we are trying to explain.

If you manage to extract anything at all out of this confusion, the chances of it telling you anything reliable are negligible. Anyway, it's much more likely, given what we said earlier, that international expansion would be found to explain profit growth, rather than profitability ratios. And if we want to be sure this is valuable growth, rather than just added scale, we should look at free cash flow.

Everything explains performance

In spite of its limited usefulness as a focus for strategic management, profitability in one form or other has featured as the dependent variable — the factor we wish to explain — in thousands upon thousands of academic papers. Moreover, most of these papers claim that their statistical analysis supports their hypotheses as to what causes profitability. So, as a result of all these fine investigations, we now know the right price to set, the right amount to spend on training, the right investment to make in cost reduction, and the right number of products to offer, salespeople to employ, customers to mail, and windows to have in our offices. Some hope!

If there's a number for something, someone has almost certainly proved that it explains profitability. All *you* need to do is find the right research paper for any decision you might take and look up the answer. But it's all nonsense. Every single one of these findings is complicated by dozens, even hundreds, of other factors involved, and there is no exact equivalent to your situation to be found anywhere.

Some smarter researchers have realised that profitability isn't a useful performance outcome to investigate and have looked for something else. Total shareholder returns (TSR) might seem a good alternative. This is the sum of all dividends received for each dollar invested, plus any increase in stock value over a substantial period of time. But TSR introduces a whole other problem: the mismatch between share price and likely cash flow. It would only work if investors always got their estimation of future cash flows exactly right, which they never do. Amazon.com's stock price jumped from less than $10 in 1998 to over

$80 in early 2000 (the year of huge losses), then fell back to less than $10 in 2001, just as it was about to become profitable. It still languished at less than $40 in early 2007, after four years of healthy cash flow. So, your research would be trying to explain how unsuccessful Amazon.com had been, by destroyingTSR between 2000 and 2007, not how it had grown healthy cash flows.

The wierdest measure of all?

Profitability and shareholder returns are not the only measures on which strategy research focuses; researchers can get excited by some quite bizarre concepts. One example is Tobin's q, defined as the ratio of a firm's market value to the replacement cost of its assets. Much academic ink has flowed in explanations as to why some firms might have a better q than others.[13]

The idea seems to reflect something our friends in finance have demonstrated: that stock markets are efficient, so that any information about a firm's future performance is reflected in its stock price. This finding seems to have been extended to the absurd idea that the stock market has perfect foresight about firms' earnings, and any firm's value at any time is an accurate reflection of what its future earnings will be. Try telling that to anyone who invested in Tyco or WorldCom, or in any of the fatally damaged banks in the run-up to 2008.

Why, in any case, should there be much significance in the ratio between the value of a firm's stock and the replacement cost of its assets? It has been clear for many years that a large and growing fraction of the economy is driven by services that require little or nothing in the way of fixed assets, and by products and services whose value reflects intangible factors like brand and reputation. In addition, firms adopt all kinds of different tactics that will interfere with any insights that might be drawn from this ratio: leasing rather than owning assets, outsourcing various activities, and so on. Nevertheless, hundreds of researchers continue to pore over the nuances of the virtually meaningless measure, Tobin's q.

Why should you care about what these folk get up to in their darkened rooms, glued to their computer screens? Two reasons. First, sooner or later, *you* pay for it. Although much research funding comes from government and private foundations, money from MBA and executive education course fees also goes to support the infrastructure that keeps all this activity going. Second, you should care because much of what you are told in courses, articles, and books about strategy reflects supposed findings from this research. So if wrong-headed research ends up telling you it's best to do something dumb, your organisation suffers.

Perhaps there's a problem with the methods we use?

"Correlation is not causation!" Every new PhD student in management has this message imprinted on their brain from the day they embark on their studies. (The arrival of storks may correlate with birth rates, but it doesn't mean that storks bring babies.) But somehow this dire warning is forgotten as those same individuals proceed to correlate anything with everything — *and* get the results published in the strategy journals.

To guard against this problem, we need to bear in mind that decent theory must not just answer the question of what causes what, but also **how**.[14] In medicine, for example, as soon as statistics suggest that a certain substance, behaviour or characteristic of patients is correlated with good or bad health outcomes, the search starts for the biological pathway by which those causes actually lead to those outcomes. Disreputable practitioners do not bother with that step, and simply claim that their wonder-treatment works, citing anecdotal cases and spurious statistics to prove their case.

Research papers in strategy commonly discuss the causal pathways that could plausibly exist, in the lead-up to listing hypotheses that their analysis aims to test. Each hypothesis describes what the researchers expect to find and explains the mechanisms by which they believe that causation should arise. Often, these hypotheses are based on the results of previous research carried out by others. This time, they may well include more data to try to improve confidence in the results or perhaps analyse data on a new situation to see if the results are transferable. In this era of "big data" when companies can and do collect truly vast amounts of information, the opportunities for statistical analysis are multiplying hugely. An unfortunate consequence this offers is the opportunity to go back and redo studies of the past, with the real possibility that more data will show their findings do not hold water.

The hypotheses will be followed by details about the method of analysis the researchers intend to follow and accounts of the data they will use, either from existing databases or collected from questionnaires or other investigations of their own.

The next step is to apply statistical tools to the data. If the researchers' suspected causal factors show a significant correlation with the performance measures they seek to explain, they claim that their hypotheses are supported. In reality, all it shows is a coincidental relationship or "casual causality" as it is affectionately termed, so the most we might say is that the hypothesis has not been disproved.

Although profitability, as we have seen, dominates the questions that strategy research investigates, it is not the only target for research. Many other factors get their share of attention, too. We might want to know, for example, whether certain strategic choices lead firms to have a strong product range, retain skilled executives, or integrate their acquisitions successfully. Whatever the question, though, you can be sure

I think this speaks for itself gentlemen...

that correlation will feature prominently in the search for an answer. Regrettably, this abuse of correlation also features in less reputable consulting studies. The analysts will skewer the data in a statistical soup, leaving the reader with the impression that some claim of causality is valid.

Unfortunately, not only does the existence of correlation not prove that X causes Y, the lack of correlation does not prove that the causality doesn't exist. The reason for this is fundamental, universal, and hugely important. It goes as follows.

Simpler is better

There is one particular feature that many established relationships in other fields seem to share: they are essentially simple. Whether we are looking at major scientific theories such as gravitation, evolution, or plate tectonics, the science behind important specialties such as aeronautics or genetic engineering, or professional procedures such as double-entry bookkeeping or litigation, there is often a very simple principle at their heart. This observation lies behind the principle of Occam's Razor, named after the fourteenth-century philosopher William of Occam.

The principle can be summarized as "the simpler the better". When we are faced with a number of different explanations for something, the simplest and most concrete is most likely to be correct, and we should only go looking for more complex or arcane explanations when the simple one has been shown to fail. And simple explanations are likely to involve readily understood factors and concrete processes, not abstract concepts and mystical processes.

Things develop!

Many important decisions and choices are not expected to improve profit results immediately, but aim to build up and hold onto things that will increase future performance. Hiring and retaining skilled staff is an obvious example, as we saw in the cases of Infosys, Shell, and RWE in Chapter 1. Product development and training are other examples. Now some of these things can be gathered together quickly; a price cut might win you more customers next week, for example. But others take years or even decades to put together, such as staff experience or complex products.

So although today's performance reflects what you *have* today, this is stuff you have collected over many years. You could, for example, be getting efficient production from staff you hired 20 years ago, or sales and profits from a product you developed 20 years ago. So it was your hiring and product development spending *then* that explains that little piece of your performance today, not what you spent this year or last.

This is not simply the delayed causality that research analysis already recognizes; today's performance *also* reflects the hiring, product

97

development, training, and so on you did ten years ago, or five, or just last year. How you are doing today reflects the entire history of your company's choices and decisions.

The implications of resource accumulation is serious!

Statistical analysis across a large sample of firms could easily find, for example, no correlation between marketing spend and sales, because it takes time to win the customers who will eventually give you the increased sales and profits. An obvious tactic to deal with this is to see if the outcome of interest correlates with the presumed causal factor at some time in the past – its lagged value. But even correlation-centric thinkers acknowledge that confidence in such lagged analysis decays, the further out in time you go, simply because more sources of random variation creep in.

But it gets worse—your analysis could even seem to confirm the **opposite** causality to what is actually happening: for example, when higher marketing spend coincides with lower profits. Marketing is costly, so management could easily decide that more marketing doesn't work. Before its benefits show up, high marketing spend corresponds with low profits, simply because of its cost. Management might then cut marketing, before the benefits that it *would* have delivered actually come through. So low marketing spend appears to correspond with high profitability.[15]

You might think this kind of misreading of the statistics is unlikely, and in such a simple case, any curious researcher would immediately try to see why such a dumb result was happening. The trouble is that there are dozens of such effects taking place across all parts of the business all the time—in hiring and retaining staff, building capacity, developing products, marketing, and sales—and all of these feature strong causal relationships that embed what has happened in the past, often over many years of history. Unfortunately, this state of affairs totally undermines what can be confirmed by simple statistical methods. (To be fair, this problem is not unique to research in strategy, or even in management generally. It pervades all the social sciences. But sharing the same error as everyone else does not make the error go away).

Admittedly, management make most of their decisions and choices without the benefit of statistical analysis. But this offers little comfort. Managers run a big risk of coming informally to the same kind of conclusions about what causes what as the academics do. We can only guess at the number of *really* bad decisions that are made because management don't understand the long-term build-up or decline of important resources or dangerous threats.

This is all pretty unfortunate, given that correlation studies so dominate strategy research. Take the conferences organised by the Strategic Management Society,[16] an organisation that portrays itself as *the* professional body in the strategy field, bringing together academics, businesspeople, and consultants. If you look at what gets presented in the sessions at its conferences, you might get a clue as to why this has happened.

Paper after paper is presented by researchers who claim to have discovered that some correlation confirms their belief about what causes what in particular cases. Executives and consultants are not so dumb as to place any faith in such findings, so they have drifted away over the years. The last such conference I looked at had over 400 participants. How many of them were corporate executives? Fewer than 30, and none of them senior, apart from the keynote speakers who flew in and out. How many partner-level strategy consultants at the conference? Sponsors apart, none. What *should* be the most important opportunity for strategy professionals from across the world to examine developments in their field has become nothing more than an academic talking shop.

A real shock is that the academics have known all this for over 20 years. A seminal article in the field explains the importance of accumulating resources and their implications for how performance changes over time.[17] It makes it pretty obvious that statistical correlation is likely to be more or less useless. The paper is amongst the most widely cited in the field, and the means for dealing with its consequences have been known for all of that time. Yet *still* these pointless studies and their meaningless findings dominate the field.

Curious about why the field persists in clinging to analytical methods that are so limited in their ability to explain anything useful, I asked

99

one of the leading figures in the field. Though he recognized the problems with statistical analysis, especially for understanding how performance changes over many years, he told me, "These methods just **are** what we do." Strategy researchers have a great big hammer and will go on for the foreseeable future bashing every question as if it were a nail.

Statistical analysis *can* be used safely, and some leading corporations do get out the big statistical guns and blast away at their mountains of data to find new insight and make better decisions. This has spawned a whole new industry, providing "business intelligence" services, or "analytics" to companies who want to make much smarter decisions.[18] But this activity is very different from the statistical studies in strategy. Typically, the tools are used to search for very local causality between tightly-coupled factors – how a tweak in interest rates affects customer sign-up for a credit card, for example, or how a detailed promotional tactic changes hotel booking rates.

Provided there is no danger of accumulation effects messing up the causality, such work is not just safe but to be encouraged. Indeed, the best companies go further and actually carry out controlled experiments to give them data about relationships that would not otherwise exist. But this is quite different from the misguided use of statistical analysis to investigate broad issues of overall business performance.

Come join our paradigm

Such behaviour among the academics may seem perplexing to outsiders. You might think that a scientific approach means a constant stream of innovative concepts getting filtered by others so that only the great ideas survive, what is sometimes called the "market for ideas." But alas, that's not quite how it works.

In any field, not just in strategy, scientists come to accept specific ideas as core concepts: think of Darwinian evolution or relativity. Colleagues in the same field then collect around these core ideas and attempt to destruction-test them, trying them out in all kinds of situations and pushing them to their limits. The better the concept survives this battering, the more it takes over thinking and research in the field, eventually becoming a dominant "paradigm". This explains a common misconception that science claims to define truth. It doesn't; it offers explanations that have not yet been proven wrong.

The paradigm survives until shown not to work. Then the hunt begins for a better explanation. Newtonian physics was fine for explaining gravitational attraction, for example, until precise measurements showed that it wasn't quite accurate enough, and relativity was born.

This process has certain advantages. Effort gets focused where there is the strongest ground for confidence, it's easiest to attract money and people for well-established questions, the idea is pushed into as many potentially useful areas as possible, and so on. What we end up with is a set of research programmes: communities of researchers concentrating their efforts on a few major related questions.

Unfortunately, there are downsides, too. Since the process sucks in most of the available cash and human resources, lesser ideas are starved. Competing ideas fare even less well; they are positively excluded, even ridiculed. When solid means of support have ceased, the dominant paradigm can launch like a ski jumper towards outer space. Since it has so much accumulated commitment behind it, major figures in the field defend the concept to the hilt, regardless of how pointless or unreliable it is. Young academics get taught by the old guard and are directed at increasingly arcane and foolish questions.

The so-called market for ideas, then, ends up being totally rigged. Only those who subscribe to the paradigm are allowed to trade, the buyers and sellers are the same people, and—as in some intellectual version of the Borg from *Star Trek*—others must be assimilated or exterminated.

Where this process has brought us to in strategy is large-scale commitment to seeking answers to the wrong questions, using methods that do not work in any case.

Have we been looking for answers in the wrong place?

So strategy research has been trying to explain firm profitability and mostly using statistical correlation to do so. Where has it been looking for the answers? A super-summarised history of the field gives an idea of the answer.

Way back in time, before the 1970s, strategy was an even more abstract idea than it is today. It had no solid principles for its foundations and was essentially seen as a craft. Business school courses were often called Business Policy and taught through case studies that were little more than journalistic stories.

This was not acceptable, though, to the universities in which the business schools were embedded. How could they be teaching a subject in a respected institution that was not a recognised academic field of study and lacked any rigorous theoretical foundations? Perhaps surprisingly, pressure came from industry itself, through the Ford, Rockefeller, and Carnegie foundations, for the business schools to become more disciplined.[19]

Academic respectability

Searching around for a recognised discipline that might have something to say about strategy, the business schools landed on microeconomics. At the time, that field was getting excited about the Structure-Conduct-Performance paradigm we remarked upon in Chapter 2, which said that industry structure (how many firms of what size) determined their behaviour (freedom to raise prices), which explained their performance (profitability). It was a shoe-in to adapt this to strategy! Although much of the economists' interest in the issue concerned competition policy—how to stop firms abusing a powerful position to rob customers—all strategy had to do was reverse the question to explain to management how they could choose and manipulate competitive conditions (though not illegally) to make better profits.

It's all about industry conditions ...

Harvard professor Michael Porter led the charge on all this, of course. It then didn't take long for other business schools to decide that they, too, wanted some theoretical rigour to their strategy courses and to adopt Porter's books for courses in both strategy for individual businesses (business unit strategy) and for multi-business corporations (corporate strategy).[20] Indeed, it was common for the new Strategic Management courses to be built *entirely* around Porter's books.

... or maybe not

This trend lasted well through the 1980s, but then two things changed. First, teachers started thinking that there must be more to strategy than

102

just industry forces; they wanted something about what was going on inside the business, beyond basic cost and margin analysis. And they found promising ideas in sources like Hamel and Prahalad's concept of core competences.[21] The academics then started questioning just how useful the industry forces view was in any case. They discovered that industry factors did not, in fact, explain very much about why some companies do better than others. Factors to do with the business itself were more important. Michael Porter, as you might imagine, was not best pleased by this finding, but even he found similar results.[22]

So there's the first explanation for performance—industry conditions and positioning—pretty much out of the window, and with it any basis for developing and implementing strategy. In any case, like the value-curve framework we looked at towards the end of the last chapter, the answer you get about what your strategy should be is just about the same, from year to year, decade to decade, so it's not much help in telling you what to do this Monday rather than last.

As a result of this disappointment with industry factors, academic research from the mid-1990s moved its focus to understanding what these business-specific items, or "firm factors" as they are known, were all about.

Cash and people don't matter

The economists were still in the driving seat and started with one of their absolute truths. They asserted simply that nothing a competitor might copy or buy, like cash, people, or capacity, could possibly be involved in any explanation of why one company is more profitable than another. If you don't have cash, just borrow it; if you don't have people, just hire them; and if you don't have capacity, just build it.

Various factors specific to one business rather than another could have been involved, but they widened the term "resources" to encompass whatever they might find. Since the obvious, tangible items (cash, people, capacity) clearly could not be relevant, the hunt started for the non-obvious, intangible factors that would give the answer—what might be called "strategic" resources, to distinguish them from the ordinary kind. To narrow the search, researchers set criteria to determine what would make a resource strategic. It would have to be:

- **Valuable**: contributing to the profitability of the business.

- **Rare**: so that competitors would struggle to find the same thing.

- **Inimitable:** or at least difficult to copy.

- **Organisationally embedded:** connected with how the business functions.

These four factors are known as the VRIO criteria.

In the years since this effort really kicked off, there have been thousands of research papers, dozens of books, and a few attempts at articles for ordinary managers to demonstrate the power of this explanation for performance and to make it practical.[23] (Don't forget, we are still trying to explain profitability differences here, not how to grow cash flow).

The problem is that they were wrong to dismiss the ordinary, tangible things in the first place. Here is why. (Sorry, this is going to get a bit technical).

What about the Income statement?

First, the income and cash flow statements already provide a perfect explanation for profit and cash flow — assuming the accountants are competent and honest. The revenue at the top of the income statement comes from customers (an entirely clear and tangible resource). The costs are largely driven by the quantities of simple, tangible resources the business has, especially staff and capacity, and some other things, like IT systems. Other costs are driven by the acquisition of those resources — it costs money to build or buy capacity, as well as to operate it — or else are simply decisions management make to spend on useful things like marketing.

If *any* explanation for performance is to be valid, then, whether it is to do with industry-related or business factors, it must operate through the items in the income and cash flow statements and therefore through the tangible resources that drive those statements. And that applies to the academics' strategic resources, too.

This may seem a little abstract, so let's make it practical. Starbucks makes more cash flow than Costa Coffee because it has many times more customers, reached through many times more stores, and served by many times more people. The question is not about what weird and wonderful intangibles they have, but how they came to grow faster, and that is down to the decisions of their management. The intangible resources and capabilities of Starbucks and Costa are unlikely to differ much—indeed, it is entirely possible that Costa is superior on some intangible factors, like staff morale or customer reputation, but still way behind on delivering cash flow growth.

The other reason to be sceptical about the VRIO criteria is that they are often not so hidden after all. Companies like McDonald's and Southwest Airlines, for example, are entirely transparent about what they do and how. We know exactly what routes Southwest operates, between which airports, serving which customers, at what price, offering what services, and so on. In the case of McDonald's, most of it is even written down in their franchise manuals! Furthermore, in the decades that these companies have been successful, scores of clever and experienced executives have moved on, some to start similar firms, but none has come close to matching the scale and cash flow of these leaders.

Finally, even if VRIO-type resources were the answer, we would have a heck of a job doing anything with them because (as we discussed in Chapter 2) the language used to define them is arcane and inconsistent, and the research rarely tries to measure them in any rigorous way, relying instead on proxies.

So there's the second explanation for superior performance out of the window, too.

None of this has stopped the academics continuing to beaver away in their quest for this Holy Grail. They dismiss any simple explanation for performance differences out of hand, simply by asserting that these must, in turn, be explained by something more subtle hiding in the undergrowth—if only we could find it.

Maybe we shouldn't use tools at all

So here's what we have been doing:

> **... trying to answer the wrong question**

> **... using methods that don't work**

> **... looking in the wrong place for the answer—twice!**

No wonder management has given up on strategy altogether and just does their best with whatever fad they read about next.

Indeed, some argue that strategic management and planning is pointless, even dangerous. They go on to demand that we should largely eliminate analysis from MBA and executive education, sneeringly referring to the MBA as a Master in Business Analysis.[24] (What other profession would so blatantly rubbish the basic knowledge on which sound practice depends?)

The touchstone for the iconoclastic view that working things out is a waste of time is the book *Strategy Safari,* recently updated but first published in 1998.[25] Each chapter describes a "school" of strategy thought: the first three defined as *prescriptive* (what *ought* to be done for the best), six termed *descriptive* (portraying what *actually* is done), and one more that purports to integrate the prescriptive and descriptive approaches. Each is claimed to be supported by an established body of knowledge.

The rationale for giving equal weight and validity to each approach is the recognition (which is correct) that most organisations do not follow a strict process of analyse—plan—implement. Instead, the book describes how most strategies are "emergent". The organisation tries out different approaches from time to time. Most of these fail and die out, becoming "unrealized" strategies, leaving whatever is left to actually happen—the "realized" strategy. This contrasts with what the authors claim is a false picture of strategy development, in which analysis leads to the creation of an intended strategy, which is then pursued deliberately and implemented.

Critically, in the descriptive approach, no emergent strategy ever becomes deliberate, which implies that management continue to make things up as they go along, for ever. There are a few problems with how the descriptive approach is presented.

All practice is not best practice. The whole premise of *Strategy Safari* is that what is done *is* just as important and useful as what would be *best* to do. You only need glance back at the small sample of cases in Chapter 1 to see the problems this assumption causes. Those failures, as well as the vast population of underachievers, are not led by people who don't think and have no general management awareness. Their leaders are mostly doing much of what the book describes. Sure, there are some failures of designed strategy, too, but deliberately continuing to do what evidence shows to be ineffective is not what a prescriptive approach to strategy recommends.

This observation of practice is used to make the case that strategy is— and crucially, it is claimed *should* be—a "craft", progressively building on touchy-feely intuition until finally the maestro can produce a masterpiece. But even in the arts and crafts, mastery of fundamental principles is virtually a prerequisite for success. Sure, the occasional gifted amateur emerges with no formal training whatsoever, but that is not the norm; top musicians will have

Try not to think of it as a cockup, think of it as an 'Emergent Strategy...'

practised their scales, cooks their proven food preparation techniques, and ballet dancers their basic steps. No one would seriously suggest lining up a random selection of amateurs and claiming that top performers should follow some distillation of what they seem to do.

But this doesn't stop the book making the case that this would actually be a good idea. It goes so far as to claim that absence of strategy can be

107

a positive virtue: "[It] need not be associated with failure…Management can send unequivocal signals [to stakeholders] of its preference not to engage in resource-consuming ceremony… [it] may ensure 'noise' is retained, without which strategy may become a specialized recipe that decreases flexibility and blocks learning and adaptation."[26] Lots of maybes here, as in so much of the make-it-up school of strategy.

Knock down the straw men. Each of the deliberate schools of strategy described in *Strategy Safari* is systematically dismantled. But in order to do this, ridiculous caricatures are set up that in no way describe the reality of competent, deliberate strategy. The "design" school of strategy is claimed to require that "one brain can handle all of the information relevant for strategy formation… [and] … that one brain is able to have full, detailed, intimate knowledge of the situation." But no one has actually claimed these requirements to be true, and nothing in the deliberate development and pursuit of sound strategy makes any such requirement, any more than one brain knows how to build an aircraft.

The "planning" school of strategy is portrayed as a distinct alternative to the "design" and other schools of strategy, and rubbished because the approach allegedly makes it impossible to adapt strategy. However, no one ever said that good strategy practice consists solely of developing a plan that is little more than a three-year budget, with no mechanism for seeking out, assessing, testing, and pursuing further opportunities.

These first two versions of deliberate strategy, along with the third "positioning" school, are then attacked with the assertion that any "design" approach to strategy separates thinking from acting—with strategy being thought out at the top but done at the bottom. But no strategically competent organisation pursuing a deliberate strategy actually does that! The information on the strategy's progress, as it is implemented, is continually fed back into the analysis and planning to adapt the strategy into the future.

"In our view, no one has ever developed a strategy through analytical technique," claim the authors. Oh, yes, they have! And this is not a question of personal view, in any case. It is an empirical question, and before making such a dogmatic assertion, which has the potential for changing the behaviours of large numbers of leaders with the power to make or break their organisations, it might be an idea to go out and check if it actually *is* true. And to check further whether analysis is a good thing or not, the strategic performance of those who do it should be compared with the performance of those who do not.

Not all deliberate strategy is documented. Implicit throughout this attack on the design school of strategy is the presumption that an organisation's strategy can only be deliberate if it is formally documented. But that need not be the case. There may be no need to write up a comprehensive document, incorporating all of the analysis, conclusions, and resulting detailed plans that support the strategy. Lack of formal documentation does not imply that no analysis has been done, no strategic position chosen, and no strategy designed. Especially in organisations with simple business models, leaders can simply get on with the continuing stream of decisions they have to take to keep the strategy on track. Skype, Ryanair, Starbucks, and others may or may not have written up formal strategic plan documents, but it is perfectly plausible that they could successfully continue to dominate their industries without doing so.

Good, deliberate strategy *includes* the other methods. A further gross distortion used to dismiss the value of deliberate strategy and promote the descriptive alternatives is that those alternatives are absent from any deliberate approach to strategy. This, too, is simply untrue.

The "learning" school of strategy is promoted as key to enabling emergent strategy. But any competent, deliberate strategy *incorporates* learning. Indeed, it may go further (though it need not) and embed learning into the formal process. The intended strategy is pursued; evidence—actual data, that is, not opinion—is sought for opportunities to enhance it; then deliberate, planned adjustments are made. Those adjustments may be small or large and may deal with underachievement of what was expected, or exploitation of better-than-expected progress. At a more fundamental level, the progress of the strategy and of competitors is explored to establish any new strategic opportunities. Then if something promising is discovered, work is done (data collected; analysis performed; plans developed) to see if that promise can be turned into reality. What is that if not learning?

The "environment" school apparently treats strategy formation as a reactive process, as though deliberate strategy takes no account whatsoever of how the organisation's environment is changing, nor of the threats and opportunities that arise from those changing conditions.

109

But no competent, deliberate strategy would ever leave out scrutiny of external developments or fail to adapt to, or exploit, them.

The "power" and "culture" schools of strategy emphasise the importance of recognising these issues if strategy is to be developed and adopted. However, any skilled leader of a deliberate strategy is going to understand and deal with these issues; it doesn't mean they have a make-it-up strategy instead.

Strategy is not art!

Every statement that strategy is an art, not a science knocks back any chance of being taken seriously by management colleagues. Such a statement comes up in just about every strategy discussion group, but it's a false dichotomy, and untrue in any case. The Picasso analogy is nonsense: not only is every work by true artists highly creative, but so is every brush stroke. Strategy is not remotely like art in this sense.

Creativity is a minuscule element of strategy (spotting that one business idea that no one else has ever thought of); 99 percent of the work of strategy consists of serious, logical thinking and working out. Even issues where creativity might be helpful are much more often tackled, successfully, by reasoning than by creative genius: you can think your way to spotting new market opportunity and work out analytically how to take on a competitor.

There are armies of strategy professionals out there (even if not named as such) doing rigorous investigation, analysis, and decision making, and helping their organisations do well as a result. Even where a genius insight happens, it will then be built on by hundreds of times more effort in its implementation than the split-second Eureka moment.

Can we please stop devaluing the vast amounts of hugely important, professional work that strategy professionals do?

Mintzberg and friends may be correct that *some* managers do in fact develop strategy in an emergent manner, never landing on a deliberate path that could plausibly deliver strong performance. That's why we have so many disasters and so much wasted effort and cash. The tragedy is that this view has been so influential that Henry has largely had his wish. Very little analysis is taught in MBA strategy classes, and virtually none in executive training.

The typical MBA would not recognise a cost curve if it hit them on the nose, nor have any clue how to construct an experience curve for the cost trajectory of a technologically intensive industry. They would have no idea how to map and quantify an industry structure to identify potential opportunities, nor how to check that a possible diversification is related strongly enough to the core business to be successful. Executives, rather than being taught any of these powerful and rigorous techniques (or at least being made aware of them so they can ask others to use them), are instead wowed with journalistic case studies, hype, and slogans.

So influential has this descriptive perspective on strategy been that it might well be the single biggest reason for the unprofessional practice of strategy that is so widespread today. The problem is that we don't know "the path not chosen". We can only speculate about how much better strategy might be practised today, how much less value destroyed, and how much misery avoided, had business schools continued to look for powerful analytical methods and reliable procedures for developing, adapting, and implementing strategy.

TIPS

- What should CEOs want out of their strategy, at least in corporate cases? A cash-flow forecast! If your strategy tools can't give you that, they are not much use.

- Ask your strategy staff, advisers (or yourself!) whether you are obsessing too much about profitability and should rather be prioritising the future strength and growth of cash flows (in monetary terms, not some ratio).

- Be very careful of any book, article, or adviser that claims some strategy insight, rule, or guideline to be reliable because it is based on solid statistical analysis. There might be some validity to the claim, but switch on your common sense, too.

- Check out whether there may be other explanations for an outcome that are more plausible and important.

- When urged to accept or dismiss some broad approach or specific method for strategy, ask yourself if the promoters of this view are representing the approach properly.

- Once again, remember that each business situation is unique, so a generalized one-size-fits-all approach will likely not provide the answers you're looking for.

Notes

1. J. L. Bower, 1996, "Research on Strategy Process: A Personal Perspective", presented at the 1996 Strategy Process Conference, Harvard Business School.

2. M. H. Hansen, L. T. Perry, and C. S. Reese, 2004, "A Bayesian Operationalization of the Resource-Based View", Strategic Management Journal, 25(13), pp. 1279–1295.

3. Paula Jarzabkowski, Monica Giuliett, and Bruno Oliveira, 2011, Building a Strategy Toolkit: Lessons from Business, Advanced Institute of Management Research. Retrieved 20-3-12.

4. C. K. Prahalad and G. Hamel, 1990, "The Core Competence of the Corporation", Harvard Business Review, May–June, pp. 79–91.

5. Malcolm Gladwell, 2000, The Tipping Point: How Little Things Can Make a Big Difference, New York: Little, Brown and Company.

6. Robert Grant. 2010, Contemporary Strategy Analysis: Concepts, Techniques, Applications, Seventh Edition, Hoboken, NJ: John Wiley & Sons, Inc., pp. 66–67.

7. Edith T. Penrose, 1959, The Theory of the Growth of the Firm, Oxford, UK: Oxford University Press.

8. See, for example, "Value and Performance", McKinsey Quarterly Special Edition, 2005, and Tim Koller, Marc Goedhart, and David Wessels, 2005, Valuation: Measuring and Managing the Value of Companies, Hoboken, NJ: John Wiley & Sons, Inc.

9. http://phx.corporate-ir.net/phoenix.zhtml?c=97664&p=irol-reportsannual

10. See Nathaniel J. Mass, 2005, "The Relative Value of Growth", Harvard Business Review, April, pp. 102–113.

11. Jim Collins, 2001, Good to Great: Why Some Companies Make the Leap…and Others Don't, New York: Random House.

12. Richard Foster and Sarah Kaplan, 2001, Creative Destruction: Why Companies that Are Built to Last Underperform the Market—and How to Successfully Transform Them, New York: Doubleday

13. McDonalds Annual Report 2002

14. See, for example, Jay B. Barney, 2001, Gaining and Sustaining Competitive Advantage, Second Edition, Upper Saddle River, NJ: Prentice Hall, Inc., pp. 59–61.

15. Clayton Christensen and Michael Raynor, 2003, "Why Hard-Nosed Executives Should Care About Management Theory", Harvard Business Review, September, pp. 66–74.

16. See Appendix 2, "Problems with Correlation".

17. http://www.smsweb.org/

18. Ingmar Dierickx and Karel Cool, 1989, "Asset Stock Accumulation and Sustainability of Competitive Advantage", Management Science, 35, pp. 1504–1511.

19. Thomas Davenport, 2006, Competing on Analytics, Harvard Business Review, 84(1), January, 98-107.

20. Rakesh Khurana, 2007, From Higher Aims to Hired Hands: The Social Transformation of American Business Schools and the Unfulfilled Promise of Management as a

Profession. Princeton, NJ: Princeton University Press. See also Malcolm Gilles' review in Times Higher Education, 12-Feb-2009.

21. Michael Porter, 1980, Competitive Strategy: Techniques for Analyzing Industries and Competitors, New York: The Free Press; Michael Porter, 1985, Competitive Advantage: Creating and Sustaining Superior Performance, New York: The Free Press.

22. C. K. Prahalad and G. Hamel, 1990, "The Core Competence of the Corporation", Harvard Business Review, May–June, pp. 79–91.

23. R. Rumelt, 1991, "How Much Does Industry Matter?" Strategic Management Journal, 12(3), pp.167–185. A. McGahan and M. Porter, 1997, "How Much Does Industry Matter, Really?" Strategic Management Journal (Summer Special Issue), 18, pp. 15–30.

24. D. Collis and C. Montgomery, 1995, "Competing on Resources: Strategy in the 1990s", Harvard Business Review, 73(4), pp. 118–128.

25. Henry Mitzberg, 2005, Managers, not MBAs: A Hard Look at the Soft Practice of Managing and Management Development, San Francisco: Berrett-Koehler Publishers. An interesting review of this book by Eric Nehrlich is available at http://www.nehrlich.com/blog/2005/01/20/managers-not-mbas-by-henry-mintzberg/. Retrieved 23-3-12.

26. Henry Mintzberg, Bruce Ahlstrand, and Joseph Lampel, 2009, Strategy Safari: Your Complete Guide Through the Wilds of Strategic Management, Second Edition, Harlow, UK: Pearson Education Limited.

27. A. Inkpen and N. Chouldhury, 1995,"The Seeking of Strategy Where It Is Not: Toward a Theory of Strategic Absence", Strategic Management Journal, 16, pp.313–323.

CHAPTER FIVE

THE MBA MYTH: WELCOME TO WIZARD SCHOOL

We can't solve problems by using the same kind of thinking we used when we created them.

Albert Einstein

Let's get one thing straight from the start: the MBA degree is **not** a professional training in strategic management. I am sure this will disappoint many current and prospective MBA students who think that strategy is *the* thing they will excel at by the time they emerge with their prized piece of paper. But it should come as no surprise to those graduates who have landed a job where they need to contribute to an organisation's strategy only to find they haven't a clue what to do.

The top consulting firms certainly don't act as though an MBA contributes anything vital. At least one of them hires bright graduates from all kinds of discipline—physics, biology, even music—and gives them all they need in a three-week mini-MBA. But you'd imagine these individuals are still at a disadvantage to genuine MBAs, right? Well, no; this firm compared the on-the-job performance of their MBA and non-MBA recruits and found no difference between the two groups.

How come the MBA doesn't equip young professionals to do strategy? For a start, most programmes feature only a single solitary core course in strategy. Others, presumably having spotted that there is nothing substantial to teach on the subject, don't even do that, offering instead a craft course called something like Business Policy. Keen students may be able to choose specialist strategy modules from their school's selection of optional courses, but few of these contribute anything resembling professional training.

To pick this problem apart, let's have a look at *who* teaches strategy in business schools, *what* they teach that passes for strategy training, and *how* that teaching is done.

Who teaches strategy?

The fact is, virtually none of the strategy professors in leading business schools have any professional experience in the field. Most have arrived via their own MBA or a degree in one of the social sciences, carried on immediately through a PhD programme, and emerged straight into a junior academic job. Along the way, they may have spent a year or two in a low-level management job or a junior analyst's role in a consulting firm. This is probably the origin of the urban myth about business school teaching: that you'll be advised by a 23-year-old PhD teaching assistant, lectured by a 26-year-old assistant professor, working with a 29-year-old associate professor, in a department headed by a 33-year-old full professor, none of whom have ever worked in a real business.

Now this might be fine if strategy had powerful and reliable methods that required expertise to acquire, that offered clear-cut answers, that could be taught by technical experts, and that you could learn by applying them and then checking your answers. Professors who have led a sheltered life in academic institutions might well acquire such technical expertise without ever going near the real world. The method experts who emerge from this process would then have a strong role to play, as they do in training for other professions.

Doctors are taught biochemistry by specialists who have never treated a patient, and architects are taught structural engineering by experts who have never designed a building. Accountants are taught the technicalities of tax by people who have never completed a company's accounts, and experts in real options and the capital-asset pricing model teach people to apply these methods to corporate finance problems. So all would be well if key methods that contribute to strategy development were taught by technical experts.

116

But strategic management, we are told, isn't like that; it's claimed to be a craft. We have been left with no choice but to adopt this position because of the weak and qualitative frameworks that pass as method in our field. There is no way of knowing whether your SWOT analysis is correct while mine is flawed; no way of ensuring that a capability analysis is sound; and no way of assessing how much innovation our business needs to undertake. All we can do is go through some broad qualitative assessment, then start trading opinions as to whose judgement we trust the most.

Not only do most strategy professors have no experience of doing strategy in practice, they also mostly—and shockingly—lack any formal education in the subject themselves. (Remember, an MBA alone doesn't qualify). How come?

Because strategic management has little in the way of theoretical foundations, other departments in business schools don't regard it as a proper academic discipline at all. A real discipline has a core of theory to which most of its members subscribe. Economics, finance and organisational behaviour can all claim as much. Anyone teaching these subjects is teaching both their theory and their practice. So to make their way up the academic ladder in strategy, many academics hitch themselves to one of those more respectable disciplines. To reinforce this preference, the strategy departments in top business schools aim to hire young academics who have a strong research and publication record, and that is more likely to be found in those other disciplines, too. As a result, strategy teaching in many top schools is actually done by economists or behavioural science specialists.

Credibility check

Try this. If you are currently taking a strategy course, whether in an MBA programme or an executive course, ask your professor if they have ever actually developed a strategy for a real organisation, lived with it for years, and adapted it as competitive conditions changed and the organisation itself developed. If the answer is no, ask in what technical strategy methods they do have expertise and whether they will teach you that expertise. Then ask what other technical skills are needed to do strategy properly and who will be teaching you those.

All this causes still further problems in what gets taught. Since strategy departments hire experts from other disciplines, the strategy teaching inevitably reflects the intellectual bias of the teacher—fine so long as they stay on their home turf, but not so hot when they have to cover other perspectives. So you might get great teaching on the behavioural aspects of strategy, say, but poor teaching on industry analysis or evaluating strategic plans. One senior strategy professor I encountered at a leading school had never come across the idea of discounted cash flow and didn't understand why one strategy with a short payback was superior to another with larger cash flows coming in later years. Since this basic concept from finance is universally recognized and fundamental to any assessment of strategic plans, this professor's classes are very likely to steer students to the wrong conclusions.

If strategy is a craft, then surely it should be taught by expert craftspeople? You only get to be expert in a craft by practising it for many years and in many circumstances. Virtually nobody teaching strategy in our business schools—*especially* in our top business schools—has any such experience in their craft. I say especially in our top business schools because that is where the obsession with academic research and publication in the most arcane journals is most dominant. Lower down the heap, schools and professors who know they can't win in the academic bear pit are more concerned with ensuring they perform well in teaching, so they hire faculty—especially adjunct faculty—who have practical experience and continuing involvement with real organisations.

To be fair, many strategy academics acknowledge the deficits in their own experience and try to fill the gap by bringing seasoned executives into class. At first sight, this guest speaker approach to strategy teaching looks a bit like the master classes in music and the arts that we sometimes see on TV. But the parallel is a poor one. In a true master class, students *perform* in front of an expert who has him- or herself performed the work expertly on many previous occasions. The maestro then takes apart the students' performance, offering constructive and detailed advice, and has them repeat key pieces of the work over and over again until they have demonstrated sufficient mastery.

Here, too, the lack of real-world experience of most strategy professors causes trouble. Because they don't know what constitutes professional expertise in strategic management, they look for speakers who are high-profile stars: larger-than-life characters who are impressive on stage and provide great entertainment. It can be real fun for the students to hear from the heroes they read about in *Fortune* magazine and the like. But what do they actually *learn* from the experience?

118

These strategy master classes are more like speeches by stars on "Great performances I have given". Question-and-answer sessions give students a chance to ask about these great performances, but they don't get to see the expert in action, and certainly don't get any coaching in the details of a real-world challenge from individuals who have themselves faced that challenge and expertly worked through it. And they certainly get no input from any of the people at lower levels who actually do the hard graft behind the strategy's headlines.

Who wants to teach anyway?

The last problem arising from academic career pressure is that it creates a huge incentive for faculty not to teach at all! Unbridled joy abounds in strategy departments when big research grants are won so that faculty can be paid to sit in their offices writing papers, rather than standing in front of a class teaching people. The research superstars can go for years with barely any contact with students or executive trainees. Ironically, this can actually have a slightly beneficial side effect. If the academics are focused on writing papers, then someone else has to do the teaching—hence the prevalence of adjunct teachers from the real world.

What Do They Teach?

Take a look around the many MBA syllabuses for strategic management that you can find on the web and you will find a number of main themes: industry analysis, sources of competitive advantage, understanding resources and capabilities, and so on. These themes are common because, as explained in Chapter 4, that is where strategy research has focused for the past twenty or thirty years.

Some MBA programmes are more focused than this, offering something that is not so much about strategy as industry forces, still promoting principles formalized by Michael Porter in the early 1980s. But we already saw that industry factors explain little of the profitability differences between firms (and that's not the right question in any case), and management have much more power to determine their own destiny than this view implies.

Nevertheless, assessing the impact of competitive forces on profitability remains an important skill for any strategy professional. Regrettably, like so much of management training, this approach has been progressively dumbed down. If you look at what students actually *do* with it in class, you find only a superficial list of competitive issues accompanied by comments about whether each has a strong, medium, or weak impact. Few students bother with any data collection or analysis to support this qualitative judgement, make any assessment of the impact on business performance, or offer any recommendations as to what management should actually do.

Given that there is a real opportunity for fact-based analysis here, even if its value is limited, how come students don't do it? There are three main reasons.

Business schools have become more customer oriented: pleasing their students has become more important than teaching and challenging them. Faculty who make students do hard work—especially if it involves numbers—get hammered on the five-point happy sheets used to collect student feedback on course quality. (I have hit that magic number a few times in the past but am frankly rather ashamed at what I did to get it!)

Teaching proper analysis is hard work for the professors themselves. It requires mastery of the method and close attention to the data. This imposes a heavy burden of preparation for classes on top of the considerable pressures to publish or perish in the other half of their professional activity.

Gurus have persuaded everyone that analysis is positively dangerous and uncool. Students and executives alike have heaved a huge sigh of relief that they don't need to bother working anything out any longer; sitting back and trading opinions will do just fine.

Little else in the strategy toolbox offers any opportunity for professors to get students to work anything out. So the rest of the core syllabus will likely require no more than some more checklists, two-by-two boxes, and pseudo-scientific attempts to rank things, such as customer needs or strategic resources (in a vain attempt to get something useful out of the resource-based view currently favoured by academics).

120

In addition to industry analysis and the resource based view, the core strategy course may feature some extra ideas, chosen to reflect the preferences of the particular department or teacher: strategy and the general manager's role, strategy implementation, the strategy process, strategy and ethics, strategy and e-business, and so on. Unfortunately, these concepts, too, have very little reliable or practical method behind them.

With so little solid theory or proven method behind strategy, teachers can take one of two approaches. They can focus on what little analysis *is* possible and try to get students to extract useful conclusions from working on case studies or their own business examples. The difficulty they encounter with this approach is that although some conclusions may emerge—say, about competitive intensity or opportunities for value creation—there is virtually nothing to suggest what the management concerned should actually do about it all.

Consensus, consensus, consensus

Alternatively, if teachers feel, as many clearly do, that there is little value in trying to analyse case study information, they can pretend that the answers will be out there somewhere in the audience and that their role as instructor involves little more than organizing and facilitating debate. The frameworks we looked at in Chapter 3 are supposedly helpful here. Instructors steer the debate by encouraging discussion along the lines they want, filling in the pieces of the argument as they go, and writing up key comments on the board—or rather *their* selection of key comments.

The most smart-arse example of facilitated class discussion I heard of concerned a professor in a top school who orchestrated a seemingly free-flowing class discussion and organized the headline comments on the board in this way, wrapping up with some powerful conclusions about what the business under discussion should do. Having thrilled the class with his masterly guided tour, he flipped the board over to show what he had written before class started: exactly the same conclusions that the class had allegedly come to all on their own. Thunderous applause all around.

There is a lethal assumption behind the facilitation school of strategy instruction: namely, that strategy will be successful so long as we can find consensus. It spills over directly into the facilitation that goes on in executive education classes and management team workshops. Consensus is regarded as the prime objective in strategy development, regardless of what the consensus actually *is*.

The danger should be obvious. If the consensus a management team arrives at is just plain wrong, their collective enthusiasm and vigour will make it even more certain that disaster will follow than if they hadn't ever reached the consensus in the first place. On the other hand, if two or three team members haven't signed up to the strategy, at least there is a chance that their foot-dragging will halt the headlong rush over the nearest cliff.

The obsession with discovering consensus often starts in the MBA classroom. Discussion of case examples will go back and forth, with the instructor distilling on the board the emerging collective view. We who have been there know what happens: one or two loud-mouthed individuals start pushing a particular view, it starts to take over the discussion, and before you know it, the entire class has come to agree on some broad answer. The danger, of course, just as when similar characters lead companies, is that strong personality can override sound reasoning. The strong instructor may not let this happen and instead steer the class towards the supposedly right answer by subtly (or not so subtly) ignoring, rejecting, or rubbishing other views.

Such situations can often degenerate into a power struggle between the instructor and one or more groups in the class. I still remember a class from my own MBA, late in the programme when the class members had developed resistance to being pushed around by the professor. After a couple of hours' discussion and some highly persuasive arguments by one or two of us (myself included, to my shame), we all agreed on a course of action. Only when the instructor revealed what happened next in that particular story did we realize just how ridiculous our collective answer had been.

Before moving on, we should redress the balance a little by recognising that there are some outstanding strategy teachers out there—not just in the sense that they get plaudits and high ratings from their students, but that they do so whilst demanding serious investigation and imposing tough challenges in class.

122

You may or may not know that business school instruction, especially in strategy, relies on an approach known as the case method. A typical strategy course will use the discussion in each class over the course of a semester to apply a particular concept to a case study of a real organisation. Before each class, students read about the week's topic in the textbook and perhaps supplement it with other articles. They then have to analyze the case they have been assigned using the approach set out in the book and come to class ready to recommend a strategic plan for the organisation. They may be called on to give their answers, and shame on anyone who isn't ready to show they have done the analysis or who can't mount a confident defence of their recommendations.

But it's all a charade. You can't say anything meaningful about a real strategy for a real organisation after so little effort, using limited data, in a 90-minute discussion among 50-odd people who have never even seen a real company. The best you can hope for is a short list of provisional conclusions about a few issues that might need to be taken into account in developing the organisation's strategy. So why, then, does the case-based approach dominate management teaching, especially in such a complex and multidimensional topic as strategic management?

It all goes back sixty years to the view prevalent at Harvard in the 1940s that:

> "The work of a graduate school of business. . .must be aimed
> at fitting students for administrative positions of importance.
> The qualities needed by business people in such positions are:
> the ability to see vividly the potential meanings and relationships
> of facts, both those facts having to do with persons and those
> having to do with things; capacity to make sound judgments
> on the basis of these perceptions; and skill in communicating
> their judgments to others so as to produce the desired results
> in the field of action. Business education, then, must be directed
> to developing in students these qualities of understanding,
> judgement, and communication leading to action."[1]

This belief managed to survive the big take-over of strategy by the academic rigour brigade. It has been swallowed hook, line and sinker by every serious business school ever since, especially when it comes to their teaching of strategy and business policy. Unfortunately, only the easy bits have found their way into most class teaching. In particular, "judgement" has been taken to mean gut instinct, rather than the conclusions that emerge from working things out; and the emphasis has been on persuading others of our qualitative assessment, rather than on coming to a shared understanding of what the factual information about a situation should be telling us. It is as though we built suspension bridges on the basis of what experienced bridge builders *felt* to be right, rather than what an analysis of loads, stresses, and cable specifications dictated was necessary.

Dissension in the academy

Not everyone is happy with this state of affairs, even in the hallowed halls of academe. Professor Michael Jensen of Harvard Business School and strategy consultants Monitor, for example, points out that this view of the case method:

> "... leaves out a critical part of what must be a theory of learning in the case [method] or any other method: that is ... the criteria to be used in 'making sound judgments'. I believe the answer to this is scientific method, the process by which we state our theories of cause-and-effect relationships and by which we test whether they actually describe the way the world behaves... all purposeful behaviour requires the use, either explicitly or implicitly, of theories that define the relation between actions and outcomes. Thus, I conclude there is no other answer to the criteria for use in 'making sound judgments' than science. This simple addition to the notion of the case method preserves all its motivational and learning advantages, while providing a clear criterion or process that has been tested for centuries for eliminating error."[2]

At least one respected senior figure in the field, it seems, would like strategy to share some of the rigour to be found in other professions. We just need to remember the warning from Chapter 4 that correlation is not science.

So what exactly *are* case studies, where do they come from, and how are they supposed to work? You can find endless information from numerous sources, especially the websites of those business schools that are committed to developing business cases, such as Harvard, Ivey, Darden, and Kellogg in the United States, and INSEAD in France. Case studies, however, are not all alike and come in a range of styles and sizes.

At the top end are extensive, densely detailed papers of 25 pages or more, describing situations facing large and complex organisations with the aid of many exhibits and appendices presenting much factual data. Few people appreciate the cost and effort needed to assemble such documents: a decently researched case can cost well over $100,000. Even before embarking on a new case, writers must consider the issues on which the case will focus, what analysis students will need to do to address them, what data this will require, and where the data can be obtained. This immediately exposes a problem.

Pick your message

A case study is not, as you might expect, a comprehensive presentation of every significant fact and issue facing an organisation at a particular time, nor could it ever be. That would take a whole book. Rather, in developing a new case, the author is already deciding what the point of the story is to be and how students and executives who study the case should be guided to solve it. For example, if the author decides that the key issue facing Samsung in the cell phone industry is the competitive intensity of the industry, then that's the data that will feature in the case. If he or she thinks Amazon's biggest challenge is about building abstract and indefinable resources, then that's what the information in the case will focus on. If he or she thinks Google's success is all about how the company's unique culture enables the innovation in its strategy, then that is what the description will concentrate on.

In fact, much case writing starts at the back end with the questions "What is the concept I want to put across?" and "Which business situation demonstrates this concept?" The danger is clear: the case study selects and presents the information needed to justify the point of view of the author, whether or not that view is in fact correct or important.

This perhaps explains a recent comment from a newly graduated top-grade MBA: "I came out of the strategy class understanding why it's hard to make money in the airline business, impressed by the powerful capabilities of Toyota, and full of admiration for Michael Dell and [Amazon's] Jeff Bezos, but I don't have a clue how to work out strategy for an organisation." It also helps explain the mystery of why so many academics falsely believe that their arcane ways of thinking about strategy are widely used in the real world.

Not only do academics set the curriculum, teach the methods, and assign the textbooks, they also decide what concepts will be conveyed in the case studies they use in their teaching. And to ensure that these concepts are taught properly through these cases, they write the teaching notes that tell other instructors how to put across the same principles when they use the cases in their classes. It is pretty bold to assume, with little supporting evidence, that students and executives then go off and use these approaches in the real world and derive value from doing so.

So, even with the best cases, carefully selected, specified, researched and written, MBA classes and executive coaching get pushed into selective approaches that have only the flimsiest foundation in reliable theory and virtually no real-world value. Harvard is right: wisdom can't be told. But neither can it be gleaned from short, superficial class discussions by groups with no experience of the profession, led by people who have never done strategy in practice, using approaches that don't do anything useful, illustrated by case studies conveying information that is fit for no other purpose than illustrating these pointless methods.

Journalism will do

And this applies to the *best* standard of case writing and presentation.

If you search around the various sources of case studies, including the standard strategy textbooks, you'll find few cases that are so substantial and rich in relevant data. What you get instead is a pile of short, descriptive articles about interesting situations. Just like their larger siblings, these mini-cases are chosen and written to show how the author thinks a particular concept applies in the real world. But most are entirely superficial, with no substantive information whatsoever on the organisation or its situation. How students or executives are supposed to draw any useful conclusions from these glib fairy tales is anyone's guess.

One last warning. Case studies often come with a disclaimer on the front page along the lines of "This case is not intended to illustrate either effective or ineffective management." No doubt this keeps the lawyers happy, but it's usually untrue. Cases on such firms as Amazon, Dell, Starbucks, GE, and Southwest Airlines are top of the pops in strategy classes precisely because they *do* seem to depict exemplary strategic management.

This is all very well until events reveal that the heroes and their corporations had little sound strategy or a strategy that ran out of steam when things changed. Enron and WorldCom were among the most popular case studies in the late 1990s. Curiously, these old cheerleader cases seem to have disappeared. There has been a long history of cases examining the reasons for the success of firms like McDonald's and Disney. But the cases from those glory days rarely pose questions about what could go wrong or how strategy should change to protect against possible problems. Old cases, of course, are unfashionable, so it's perhaps not surprising that the gee-whiz stories of fallen giants have dropped off the menu. But this is a pity, since we could potentially learn a lot from a forensic analysis of the strategic management errors that led to disaster.

A more honest disclaimer for most case studies might be "This case is intended to illustrate why the author thinks the management of this organisation is so smart and/or dumb (delete as applicable)."

The disappointing thing about the case study industry is just how much high-powered intellect and human capacity gets devoted to generating such useless material. Frankly, we'd be better off devoting a tenth of the effort to producing two percent of the output, but at five times the quality.

Where's the WHOLE story?

Guidelines for writing cases generally urge the writer to build the case around a single question, issue, or dilemma faced by management, or a limited related set of issues. Reasonably enough, this provides the basis for a focused debate, hopefully around important learning points that might be addressed with particular tools or methods.

Such an approach is all very well, but out in the real world, organisations have a bigger need than to answer isolated, independent questions—they have to put together a whole strategy, then deliver and adapt it. That strategy may be for the overall progress of the organisation or for dealing with a single large initiative that nevertheless poses multiple interrelated issues for all or most parts of the organisation. So where are the case studies and teaching notes to help students and executives learn how to do this?

I get a continual stream of announcements on the latest strategy cases, but not a single one could ever be used by students to carry out a comprehensive analysis on an organisation, construct a complete strategic plan, and estimate in any detail the likely future performance of the organisation. This would require a very large case study indeed, with large amounts of data, worked on progressively over many classes.

If the case studies cannot do this because they are directed at explaining a single key idea in a single class, then maybe the textbooks could do it. After all, most are designed to support at least an entire semester of classes. Surely, then, as well as the issue-specific cases, they could offer at least one case that describes comprehensively the situation of a single company with similarly comprehensive supporting data.[3] Then the book's teacher guide could explain how to get students, over the whole semester, to do the whole strategy task:

- Build up a complete analysis, using the full set of strategy methods available.

- Reach conclusions about all aspects of the organisation's situation.

- Make a complete and integrated set of recommendations as to what management should do.

- Develop a complete projection of likely future performance.

- Provide a sound set of metrics and processes for monitoring and adapting the strategy over time.

The case could even be incremental, setting out information on the state of the organisation and its market and competitive environment at one point in time, then exposing a sequence of updates.

But that is way too much to hope for. None of the many textbooks I have seen make any attempt to even approach this task. If anything, they are going the other way. Many once offered a reasonably substantial case to support the main theme of each chapter; now they increasingly seem to offer no more than one- or two-paragraph snippets that are supposed to elucidate key principles.

Where's the implementation?

The final weakness of most strategy cases and textbooks is that they have little or nothing to say about how strategy actually gets implemented. Here we do not mean the organisational behaviour stuff about getting people engaged and bought in to the strategy (though that is important, too). Instead, we mean the full, continuing set of decisions and actions taken by management, across all parts of the business, over long periods of time. It is the total sum of these choices and actions that in reality make up the realized strategy so much beloved by our friends who favour the descriptive approach to learning about strategy.

Many case studies do try to tell a story of some organisation's development, and some may highlight key choices made at particular times, but none, it seems, get anywhere close to explaining the complete set of choices and actions needed to adequately document a strategy as actually *implemented*. What might such a strategy description need to include? A full sequence of pricing changes, marketing spend, product launches, hiring patterns, capacity expansions, IT initiatives, and more. Not an easy task, to be sure, but it's all of these things that make up the full scope of a real-world strategy.

One might forgive case study writers, limited to providing something that can be feasibly discussed in a class or two, for failing to offer such a fully comprehensive strategy description. But they could at least provide enough time-based information to show how particular aspects of a strategy are implemented through the sequence of management choices—the steps taken quarter by quarter to enter a new geographic market, for example, or to target and defeat a competitor. However, time-series data is almost entirely absent from published case studies, apart from the high-level financial values in the accounting statements.

The textbooks have far less excuse for this omission. Any case examples they offer could quite reasonably be expected to set out the sequence of decisions made by the management of an organisation to deliver strategy and performance, but none do.

129

There are reasonable practical reasons why this is not done, of course. It would for sure be a lot of work and therefore expensive. It would also require the organisation concerned to be extremely open—way beyond anything they would normally share outside the boardroom. But there could just be another reason why you never see any information about how strategy is actually implemented...

Remember, as explained way back in Chapter 1, that strategy requires a business to choose a strategic "position" where it can feasibly build a strong business, and then make a continuing sequence of decisions to make it happen (adapting decisions, of course, as circumstances change). Remember, too, that the theories of strategy, such as they are, focus on explaining profitability ratios as a function of industry factors or features of the business itself. Finally, recall that the conclusions you could draw from most of the methods in the field seem to be exactly the same today as they would have been years or even decades in the past. Well, if your explanations for success, measured in these static terms, are static, too, why would you even bother to explore how the full set of decisions made across the whole business change as the strategy progresses?

Perhaps this is the more realistic explanation as to why the strategy textbooks are almost devoid of any mention of strategy implementation and certainly offer nothing methodologically sound for working out how it should be done. Success, they seem to say, simply requires you to pick the right position and identify the important resources—et voilà, as the French would say—job done!

What About the Students?

We shouldn't move on without a word or two about the students and what *they* do. Needless to say, just as there are outstanding strategy teachers, there are many outstanding young professionals in our MBA programmes: immensely bright, hugely committed, and hard-working people who produce brilliant work. But not all are this hot, and indeed the MBA system itself encourages some pretty dysfunctional behaviour.

We already noted that the MBA, like any degree, is not a professional qualification that offers defined standards of achievement. There are thousands of MBAs offered across the world at institutions ranging from the most prestigious to the downright lousy. You can even buy them by mail order! Students know all this and either try to get into the best business school they can or else just go for the piece of paper with the letters on it, regardless of standard. Employers, too, know that standards vary, so if they have any sense, they take account of the source of a job seeker's qualification.

All this gives rise to a self-fulfilling prophecy. The best schools attract the brightest applicants, who achieve the greatest mastery of business, who get the best jobs, with the best employers, for the highest salaries—all of which leads the cream of the next crop of students to follow the same well-trodden path, which creates some interesting consequences.

The GMAT Olympics

First, the financial value of a top-school MBA, in terms of future earning power, creates a big incentive for would-be students to strive to get in. Most schools use the GMAT test from the Graduate Management Admission Council to filter the standard of applicants they will accept. Because a top MBA is so valuable, a whole industry has grown up to *train* applicants to score well on the GMAT—not just in the US, but around the world. This was probably inevitable given the MBA market structure but makes nonsense of the idea that we are choosing students on the basis of their fundamental ability. The GMAT is a structured testing scheme, and doing well at it is something you can be trained to do.

You might argue that people can be trained only up to a ceiling set by their innate intellect, but faculty I have spoken to aren't so sure. Although most students entering good schools seem able (even if they are rarely required) to do work that is consistent with what their GMAT score would suggest, many are not. Even in the premier league of business schools, some students are just plain dumb, unable to follow the simplest instructions or solve the most trifling problems.

How this happens is a mystery. Perhaps training really can get applicants to give answers that are much smarter than they would normally be able to produce. There have also been allegations of fraud, such as GMAT-rigging groups. GMAC and the business schools undoubtedly take all this very seriously and strive to protect their systems' integrity, but it's hard to guard against every devious scheme and to know how prevalent cheating may be.

131

It seems that some students will stop at nothing to get into the best schools. One professor told me about a student who turned up at the start of the course but didn't quite seem to match the person who had gone through the application process. The person interviewed in the country of origin had been a woman, and the student who turned up was a man!

Once through the gate …

Once students get into the school of their dreams, other factors kick in. Some of them get the idea that having made it this far, they don't need to do much more before grabbing the award at the end. A student in one of the world's top ten schools objected to being given a C grade for a truly useless performance throughout a strategy class: he couldn't possibly be so weak, given his impressive GMAT score and the fact that he was a McKinsey consultant. (If it had been my decision, he'd have failed.)

Many students look for ways to play the system and spot immediately that hardly anyone ever fails or gets dismissed from their course. On the very few occasions it does happen, students often call the nearest lawyer, so schools rarely have the nerve to point out that someone is just not up to the required standard. Instead, they "manage" the weakest through to the end of the process. In any case, it isn't a good advertisement for a school's degree if they are seen to be throwing out people they originally accepted. (And let's not forget those course fees!)

Approaches to grading students' work vary widely. Many schools operate a letter-grade system running from A down to C, maybe with plusses and minuses to make finer distinctions. You might expect this to create a degree of comparability among MBA grades. Far from it. Since there are no set standards as to what constitutes quality in any grade, certainly none that are open to public scrutiny, grade inflation is rampant. Overall, B is often supposed to mean below average, but in some schools *everyone* expects to get an A. Several top-school graduates have told me that all students in some classes could guarantee themselves A grades simply by taking part in a professor's research activities.

The forced-curve

In an effort to bring a bit of discipline to this mess, some schools operate a so-called forced curve to impose a standard distribution of grades among the students. For example, half must get A grades and half B or below. This policy is undoubtedly well intentioned. If you *don't* enforce a grade distribution, instructors are tempted to give high average grades to ensure the popularity of their class, especially if it is optional. Another argument for the forced-curve policy is that it should encourage the students to scramble to outdo one another for a place at the top of the heap, thus driving up standards. This works for some, but it also has some unfortunate side effects. After a while, good students realize they can't do any better no matter how hard they try, so they revert to doing just enough to get by. What happens on the bottom end of the curve is still worse: students catch on that they won't get too bad a grade no matter how little they do and so submit truly dismal work.

In the worst cases, an entire class can end up playing the system. One professor told me about a class he gave where none of the students had bothered doing the reading or preparing the case study. Since my friend couldn't get on with the course until this material had been properly prepared, he cut the class early and sent the students away to do the preparation they were supposed to have done. The following week, he was shocked to find that most of the students still hadn't done it. After class, he asked one of them why. "Well, you have to mark us to a forced curve anyway," the student replied. "So what are you going to do about it?"

What do students actually produce?

Once again, let's be fair: students' best strategy work can be outstanding, and the effort and intellect that goes into MBA assignments can be remarkable. Again, though, this shining pinnacle sits atop a mountain of mediocrity in a swamp of the most appalling garbage. Even in our best schools, students get away with superficial journalism in place of soundly reasoned arguments and powerfully compelling conclusions. How come?

The explanation goes back to the lack of professional experience among faculty. If you have never seen professional strategy work, let alone had to produce any yourself, you won't know how to set rigorous standards for the students you instruct. This is not much of an excuse, in fact; even if we aren't champion figure skaters ourselves, we should still be able to tell when beginners keep falling over. It would seem not. Ordinary folk would be shocked at the weak assignments that don't just scrape a passing mark but get A grades, even in our leading schools. And don't presume, by the way, that the best work comes from the best schools, and that students from lower-ranked institutions don't do good stuff. I've seen great work from keen and able students in tertiary colleges, and trite nonsense from Harvard whiz kids.

Many faculty should really ask themselves, "Would I be happy to take this student to the management of the business they are writing about and try to persuade them that they should do what my student is recommending?" If not, the assignment should be failed—except, of course, that no one does fail. All this gets to be a vicious spiral: students do poor work, which gets passed by faculty who know no better, which sets poor standards for work by the next cohort of students to come through the system.

What's to be done?

There are feasible solutions to all this. We could start with those case studies. The best among them come with teaching notes advising how to use the cases in class. We should expect more: namely, model answers offering a persuasive analysis, conclusions, and recommendations that tackle the issues in the case and propose solutions that are both strategically powerful *and* safe against likely eventualities. Ideally, these model answers should be endorsed by the managements that have experienced these situations, who should agree not only that the model answers are sound, but also that they deal with the real issues in their business and aren't just examples of standard analysis using irrelevant frameworks. This solution comes with its own problems, of course.

There is already a thriving black market in case teaching notes and we could probably expect a similar market in model answers to appear overnight.

We could at least expect schools to publish examples of student work, divided by exceptional (A+), good (A), acceptable (B), and unacceptable grades. Such an arrangement would clearly need to be made explicit in an agreement between schools and students when they enrol in their MBA, but there would be no need to infringe upon students' privacy. Faculty could even concoct sample papers themselves at each grade level and publish them on their school's MBA website.

Lastly, employers could exert pressure by asking to see a portfolio of applicants' work from throughout their degree. As a final MBA assignment, some schools expect students to demonstrate their expertise in general management by means of an integrative project, often a kind of mini-consulting exercise for a real organisation. Employers could ask to see these reports. This would be revealing because some schools at least try to make sure such projects are of genuine practical value to the organisations that sponsor them. In its guidance to students and supervising faculty, one school emphasizes that whether they use anything learned from their MBA programme to carry out the assignment is entirely up to them!

After the initial shock that many will experience upon seeing the irrelevance and shoddiness of much that students produce, organisations that hire MBAs may at least be clearer about what exactly they are buying when they shell out those fancy salaries.

By now, you may well share some of my gloom at the dismal state of the strategy field: not just in the poor strategic management we all see in the organisations we know, but also in the useless methods that are supposed to help executives avoid these errors and the hopelessly superficial education that is supposed to support the profession. There is indeed a mountain to climb if we are to create something that approaches professionalism in the field.

But all may not be lost. There are ways to improve things, and we will look at some of these opportunities in Chapter 6.

TIPS

For students:

- Before signing on to a degree program, check out the quality of the institution. The best are accredited by the Advanced Association of Collegiate Schools of Business (AACSB) or the European Foundation for Management Development's Quality Improvement System (EQUIS).[4]

- Many non-accredited schools may nevertheless teach strategy well, especially outside North America and Europe. The standards set a host of diverse criteria, and the accreditation process is very costly, so a good course may still be found in non-accredited schools. You will just need to be extremely diligent in checking the course content.

- Beware that many accredited schools teach strategy badly, by teaching useless concepts, having no connection to how strategy is best done in the real world, or both.

- Check the curriculum and ask exactly what it covers; if the school won't tell you, look elsewhere.

- Check the career and educational credentials of those who actually teach the courses—not the top professors, who you will likely not see in any case, but the juniors. You can even call them up and ask what they teach and how. If they can't or won't tell you, look elsewhere.

- Once enrolled, select the courses that actually teach you how to do useful things. These courses may not even be in the strategy department; powerful methods of real value for strategy can be found in marketing, finance, operational research, and other departments.

- Look for opportunities to do real strategy assignments, and keep your best work to show employers. Seek permission to do so from any real-world organisations you get to practise on.

For faculty:

- Check that you understand and can deploy the full core set of methods that any foundation course in strategy should cover. (This will take a bit of work in itself, since there is no definitive source of these basic skills; you certainly can't get it by going through a single textbook.)

- If you can't gain a comprehensive understanding of strategy, decide what exactly you do know and can teach that is of real value, and focus on that. Don't pretend you know more than you do.

- Look for cases and teaching materials that provide you with comprehensive information on how to teach rigorous methods; amongst the mountain of content-free material out there lies a small proportion of genuinely useful stuff.

- If you have no practical experience of strategy, by all means bring in real-world speakers, but go for the solid professionals who actually run the strategy process in organisations – not the glitzy CEOs.

For recruiters:

- Demand to see the content of what students are taught about strategy.

- Demand to see the standards against which students are assessed.

- Always insist on seeing a good sample of students' work, especially real-world assignments.

- If you don't like what you see – especially if it is clearly irrelevant to real-world strategy – complain over and over again. The schools won't change if no one demands it.

- If sending executives on open strategy courses, go through the same checking process as listed above for students. (The best practice for commissioning tailored courses for your organisation is a much bigger topic, worth a chapter or two on its own!)

Notes

1. Charles Cragg, 1940, "Because Wisdom Can't Be Told", Harvard Alumni Bulletin, 19th October.
2. Michael C. Jensen, 1999, "The Case Method and Science", Social Science Research Network. Retrieved 28-3-2012.
3. An example of a serious case-study, with enough information to enable students to carry out a series of strategy analysis tasks as part of several classes, concerns the European low-fare airline industry. This case is built entirely from public information – a focused case on a specific company could go into much greater depth.
4. Links for these organisations are http://www.aacsb.edu/accreditation/ and http://www.efmd.org/index.php/accreditation-main/equis.

CHAPTER SIX

WHAT'S TO BE DONE?

The society which scorns excellence in plumbing as a humble activity and tolerates shoddiness in philosophy because it is an exalted activity will have neither good plumbing nor good philosophy…neither its pipes nor its theories will hold water.

John W. Gardner (1912–2002), president of the Carnegie Corporation

OK, so there's a big problem. How can we fix it? We have a few options. We could chuck the lot, do nothing, fix what we can, or try to establish a genuine strategy profession.

Chuck the lot

Imagine reading this in the Financial Times in 2020:

At Last: The Death of Strategy

So the business schools have finally seen sense. This month saw the last school drop strategy from its MBA courses, while another was the last to discontinue its executive course in the topic. They have eventually accepted the reality that the world is so uncertain that there's no point trying to work out the best thing to do, so managers should save themselves a whole lot of time and not bother trying. As we all know, shooting from the hip is just fine, provided you shoot fast and scatter your fire across a wide enough range.

Since the methods strategy claims to offer don't work, people stopped using them years ago. Management education never equipped executives to develop and manage strategy, so there was no point taking courses on the subject, at business school or anywhere else. No MBA taught anything useful about strategy, so students avoided classes on the topic and went to classes on leadership instead, learning to emulate the brilliance of top executives, reported on in this newspaper and elsewhere, who make up their organisation's strategy as they go along.

Dropping strategy from executive education and MBAs will help the academics, too, freeing them up to research and write about still more issues that are of no interest or use to management. This will also be good for the publishing world. They will get more new books on daft ideas and more esoteric articles to flummox management and add to the mystique of the strategy gurus.

Top managers never did waste much time and energy on educating themselves about strategy, so now they will be saved from any embarrassment that there might be something missing from their expertise. Freed from this uncertainty, they can get on still faster with making ill-judged decisions and pursuing foolish initiatives. They will be able to waste still more of their investors' money and do still more harm to the livelihoods of the people who work for them and to the wider economy.

With no need to show they know what they are doing, the strategy consultants will be free to come up with more innovative plans for businesses to rush into and charge still more money for their advice, and no one will be any the wiser. Or management may become confident enough to mess up all by themselves and not bother hiring consultants to tell them how to do it in a more spectacular fashion.

Hmm? Perhaps this is not the best future we could imagine.

High-performing organisations *do* work out where good opportunities lie and how to build the resources, capabilities and operational excellence needed to capture them. So telling management to stop putting in all this effort and start making things up as they go along may not be too clever—even though some experts seem to be advocating precisely that.

Ignoring strategy tools that don't work or are easily misused may not

140

be a bad idea. After all, that's pretty much what we do already. But at least these tools encourage executives to *think* about stuff. Even if their thinking is often flaky, they may start to apply common sense to some decisions and avoid doing too many dumb things.

We should certainly stop using consultants, right? Everybody knows they employ overpaid youngsters who know nothing about your business to make ill-judged recommendations for changes that only cause damage, and then take no responsibility for the harm they do. Well...no. The good ones know things that you don't and can do things that you can't. At a time when management as a whole has very thin strategy expertise, consultants are the best repository we have right now for anything approaching professionalism.

The MBA seems a pretty pointless piece of paper, with its non-existent standards, feeble content and process, and inability to give future executives much in the way of useful skills. But it would be rash to chuck it out, for the same reason given above: it at least encourages folk to think about what to do, even if the methods aren't up to much. And the alumni who are out there now are a community of *potential* professionals who have a stake in making things better. If we let that community dissipate, things are not likely to improve.

We've seen the problems that arise from the lack of real-world exposure among academics. So if we really wanted to make things worse, we could insist that they stay away altogether from businesses and the executives that run them. A real pessimist might see some benefit in this: at least management could spend the time they currently waste talking to academics on doing something useful instead. They would also be spared the worst of the damaging ideas that emerge from the ivory tower. "Do nothing" is often a pretty good option—better than messing things up by trying something dangerous or inappropriate.

But leaving the academics to devote themselves *entirely* to arcane research and meaningless articles for each other in journals that no one else reads won't do either. There's a lot of good stuff in there somewhere; we just need to tease it out, put some effort into it, and turn it into something practical.

Simple though it might seem, the knee-jerk reaction of throwing all that strategy stuff out of the window and going by gut instinct alone could quite easily make matters worse.

141

Do nothing

Perhaps we should change nothing at all? By and large, US businesses continue to thrive and support the world's largest economy—for now. The US remains the home of the largest number of sector-leading global firms, as well as most of the fastest-growing new enterprises. By adopting many of the principles that have long featured in US management practice, European corporations and increasing numbers in developing economies are doing OK, too. But the strategy community can take little credit for this. Corporate success seems to have little to do with any mastery of strategic management; instead, the credit lies more with the flexibility of our economies, the potency of our technological resources, and the energy and entrepreneurialism of our people.

These advantages may not last, though. The spectacular emerging business sectors of India, China, Brazil, Turkey, and other countries are starting to share them, too. Manufacturing industries have already seen what happens when competitors from the Far East display an annoying ability to work out how best to do things and then make it happen. With their increasingly well-educated management, enterprises from that entire region can be expected to apply the same discipline and determination to developing the strategies of their businesses that they have already applied to establishing operational excellence.

So doing nothing is not the way to go. Worse still is the "do less" option promoted by some gurus, who seem to think that business schools spend too much time teaching folk how to work things out, and want them turned into craft schools instead. Sure, there is much craft in management, but building strong and sustained business performance also calls for rigour and intellect..

Unfortunately, "do nothing" seems the most likely prospect right now. As psychologists know, people faced with any severe shock—bereavement, divorce, redundancy, and so on—typically go through several stages. First comes denial, followed by anger, bargaining, depression, and ultimately acceptance.

The strategy community, especially its researchers, teachers and writers, seems permanently stuck in the first phase, stoically insisting that all's well with the world and burying their heads in the sand. Like an employee about to be laid off who can't accept that what they do is superfluous,

142

the community keeps up the pretence that their activity is useful. The rest of us don't help. By reading their books, going to their classes, and seeking their advice, we allow them to carry on as normal, sustaining the illusion.

Improve what we can

The lack of any professional infrastructure limits the scope to improve the present shambles of strategic management. Yet we are not entirely powerless. Each of us can contribute to raising standards.

Senior management: Get a grip

Top executives clearly have the central role in improving the situation. Nothing much is going to change unless CEOs are brutally honest about their own professionalism. Do you *really* understand your organisation's strategy and how it is evolving as market and competitive conditions develop? Do you *really* have a rigorous quantitative understanding of how changes in the main parts of your business interact to drive your performance? Do you *really* understand the nature and scale of change in your markets and channels? Do you have any *real* idea what your competitors are up to, what impact their actions will have on your performance over time, and precisely what you should be doing about it? Is your understanding of these issues based on solid facts and constantly updated with new information, not just crude financials?

Unless you answer yes to all of these questions, you don't have a professional grasp of strategy and you should get yourself trained. But finding quality training in strategy won't be easy. So before you enrol in a class, track down people who have already taken it. Ask what usable strategy approaches they learned, how they have integrated them into the way they run their organisation, and what it has been worth in revenue and cash flow growth, or whatever other objectives they pursue. Check that the class is genuinely about strategy, not leadership (a vital topic, but different), and that instructors and speakers have actually *done* strategy in the real world.

There's no need to limit the search to business schools. There are many skilled and experienced individuals capable of coaching you and your team in the fundamental skills. But beware: there are hacks and charlatans

143

out there so be sure to go through a careful checking process. And tap into your personal networks and other professional groups to find the good people who can help you.

Up-skill others

Investors and employees might at least expect CEOs and strategy VPs to be familiar with everything of potential value from sources like this. But it's not enough for these two individuals alone to understand strategy; the members of their teams can't make meaningful contributions unless they too understand the basics. CEOs will probably be pushing at an open door if they invite their VPs of human resources, marketing, IS, and production to be trained in strategy. People in functional roles often feel frustrated that they don't know how to contribute to their organisation's overall strategy. And it isn't good enough, as one strategy textbook puts it, that functional managers "must be told which higher-level strategies have been chosen and then tailor functional-area strategies accordingly." Strategic management is a *continuous* and *two-way* process between overall direction and functional elements.

Don't forget, either, that in our fast-changing world, we can't afford to wait for every potentially strategic decision to go up to the top team and down again before anything gets done. Each business team needs at least one strategy professional. And we should encourage these folk to build a community of professional practice in strategy. Most functional executives have like-minded colleagues working for them, but it can be lonely if you are the only strategy person around. Get these folk together so they can help each other identify, learn, and adopt strategy methods that might be useful for your organisation. Some major corporations already take this issue seriously. Defence firm BAE Systems, for example, employs over one hundred people in strategy roles, and works hard to develop and sustain their collective capability.

When you operate in a constantly changing environment, it's surely time to drop the idea of strategy as an annual ritual, absorbing huge amounts of everyone's time for a few weeks and then being shelved until next year. Would you do strategic plans every 800 days rather than 365, if that's how long it took for the earth to go around the sun? Develop a living plan, and use those monthly team meetings to check progress on the key features *and* check if anything needs changing.

144

Don't let yourself be pushed around by consultants or bankers. They of all people should be able to tell you why their proposals are powerful and safe. My consulting friends say they are astonished how little interest their clients show in the rationale behind their recommendations. Yes, we know the few superstar business leaders can tell instantly if their advisers know what they are talking about just by looking them in the eye. But we ordinary mortals lack these telepathic skills and need to check. It's also important to know the rationale behind the advice you get so that you can implement it properly and adapt what you do if circumstances change.

Consultants: best practice, please

Strategy consultants themselves face a dilemma. On the one hand, they will likely get better work, and see it implemented—and implemented better—if clients have some clue as to why it all makes sense. On the other hand, if clued-in clients stop accepting proposals for pointless projects, the consultants may not get engagements at all. Those bright young things with the fancy bonuses have to be kept billable!

Nevertheless, there are a few things we might ask of them. To the worst offenders, who trample over clients for three months, dump a big report on them, and then walk away: *could you please just stop it.* The best firms go back to clients some time after projects are completed and check whether the recommendations were successfully followed through. Consultants could even go further and coach senior management in strategy, helping them accomplish the recommendations and deliver results.

A bit more honesty would be welcome, too. Why not make it clear up front that the study may not stick to a fixed schedule and prepare for it to pause while important knowledge gaps are filled in? Consultants could also check at the outset that clients have the willingness and capability to do the kind of things that may be recommended at the end. How many boardrooms have a shelf full of great consultant reports, none of whose recommendations have been carried through? Please, CEOs, stop commissioning costly consulting studies simply to demonstrate your virility!

Honesty could be extended to telling clients when it would be best to do nothing. Maybe there's even a great consulting proposition in offering

145

to tell clients how many things they can *stop* doing.

The big problem for clients is that most don't use these advisers very often and don't understand how they do what they do, so don't really know what to look for. This isn't helped by the diversity of strategy challenges that come along—which is why strategy consulting is so lucrative, compared with commodity services like auditing and IT support.

Business schools: Raise the bar

Our business schools could make a big contribution, too. They could start by being explicit about their standards, both to would-be students and to the wider business community. This applies to most of the subjects they cover but is certainly needed with regard to strategy. Business schools should share with us, fully and openly, what they regard as good strategy work and the level below which students' performance is unacceptable. Tough though it may be in our litigious world, those who hire MBAs would appreciate the reassurance that students who don't meet required standards will be failed. Sound students would have nothing to fear; indeed, they would probably welcome strong standards because such standards enhance the value of their degree and their own credibility.

Our strategy professors could also start a serious effort to clarify what there is in the field that is genuinely relevant and useful. They may well protest that it's not their job; they are the scientists and it's up to the engineers in the profession to turn their science into practical tools. But that's just not good enough. When we have had half a century of science that has made no discernible contribution, in spite of the best efforts of those engineers, it's time to question the underlying science. We need to clear out the closet. The consulting professionals have a powerful incentive to find anything of value among the detritus, so they should be only too willing to help

The challenge from then on will be to stop the garbage building up again. So the next task for the academics would be to take a hard look at their research programmes, identify any that aren't ever likely to generate anything of practical value, and stop them. If they want to pursue questions purely for the intellectual satisfaction, that's fine, but *don't* call it strategy, *don't* pester busy people with it, and *don't* swallow up research funding by claiming it's useful.

146

The same clear-out will need to be done to the strategy teaching materials: textbooks, cases, and exercises. By the time you've stripped out the abstract, ambiguous, and unproven checklists, two-by-two boxes, and frameworks, there's not much left of a strategy textbook. But some content is based on rigorous foundations and will need rewriting to show how it can be used in a fact-based manner to solve real challenges for real organisations. Drop the descriptions of how tools *might* apply to case studies and replace them with real examples of how they *were* used by real people to make important decisions that delivered real value.

Weed out the case study collections: pick out the few that contain enough real information for students to come up with professional strategy proposals, and if you can't shred the rest, find a way to hide them away.

This may all be a bit threatening for younger faculty and strategy researchers, but they should console themselves with the knowledge that they will be free to do something useful with their lives. Surely they would find it more rewarding to abandon esoteric and irrelevant speculation and devote their talents to the epic task of building professional understanding and practice in strategy?

Knock down the barriers

Useful though these changes might be, there are powerful interests locked into the current situation.

Few business school professors may be keen to change anything. Their world is quite comfortable as it is, but they could be shaken into action by more direct challenges to develop strategy concepts and methods with real value. Well-informed demand from customers, both MBAs and executives, for powerful, practical learning could just force some change in the quality of strategy training they offer, too.

The leaders who achieve and sustain their status by promoting some mythical ability, then get handsomely rewarded for failing, will hardly rush to expose their ignorance. But if investors, employees, and regulators were to demand some evidence of their strategic skill, the naked emperors might just be exposed and replaced by others with serious capability. The recruitment consultants who negotiate outrageous deals for these folk have a role to play, too. They should add to their checks on leadership

147

qualities a more thorough assessment of their candidates' true strategic understanding.

Institutional investors could help here. It is quite remarkable how laid back they are about the poor strategies and foolish decisions of the corporations in which they invest our money. If they had a better grasp of the link between strategy and performance, they would be in a much stronger position to challenge what is being done.

The investment industry's dominant professional body — the CFA Institute (CFAI)[1] — could help here. It is extremely influential: so respected is its qualification program that regulators recognise the charter as a proxy for licensing investment professionals. The Institute has over 100,000 members; more than half are in North America, but the Institute has societies in 57 countries and members in 70 more, so its global influence can only be increasing.

Nearly 90 percent of the Institute's total membership holds the CFA designation[2], a certification achieved only after undertaking three levels of intensive training, based on a large and detailed body of knowledge (BoK)[3] and passing demanding examinations with a high failure rate (which is indicative of high standards). Now financial analysts are involved in many things that have nothing to do with business, such as fixed income investments and wealth management, but a large fraction of the profession works directly or indirectly on activities in which corporate performance is a critical issue. But although their training includes a few relevant topics, such as economics, corporate finance, and financial performance, there is not a word in the Institute's body of knowledge about business strategy or how it is associated with business performance.

The CFAI is therefore in a powerful position to mandate that some essential understanding of strategy and performance is a key part of investment professionals' training. The CFAI is also in a position to retrofit this knowledge amongst its charter-holders by making it a requirement of their continuing professional development. These actions would eventually get the investment industry sufficiently clued in to demand competent strategic management in the corporate sector.

Inside information

Two senior executives overheard in the men's room of a Fortune 500 company:

> *A: "What do you reckon Wall Street will think of these results?"*
>
> *B: "Well, I reckon they'll compare our SG&A [sales, general, and administration costs] with our main competitor, then we'll have to let go of another bunch of folk."*

By such "strategic" considerations are our major corporations driven!

Pressure for more professional standards of strategic management could also be applied by regulators, such as the Securities and Exchange Commission. Its regulations require listed firms to provide in their returns a "Management's Discussion and Analysis of Financial Condition and Results of Operations" (MD&A). The SEC explains:

> *The MD&A requirements are intended to satisfy three principal objectives:*
>
> 1. *To provide a narrative explanation of the company's financial statements that enables investors to see the business through the eyes of management,*
>
> 2. *To enhance the overall financial disclosure and provide the context within which financial information should be analyzed, and*
>
> 3. *To provide information about the quality of, and potential variability of, a company's earnings and cash flow, so that investors can ascertain the likelihood that past performance is indicative of future performance.*[4]

European companies and businesses in other jurisdictions face similar requirements from their own regulatory authorities.

It's hard to fulfil these objectives in the absence of any coherent, fact-based, and adaptive model of a firm's strategy, its market and competitive environment, and its prospective performance. Regulators might reasonably demand more rigour from the strategy profession so that the MD&A can be made amenable to serious, objective audit.

149

So although there may be obstacles to changing the current weak state of the strategy field, it looks like there some stakeholder groups could have both the motivation and power to demand change.

Establish a profession

While incremental efforts might conceivably improve matters, there are too many obstacles to expect much progress. If the logjam is to be broken, something more fundamental is required. We need to turn away from the amateurism of the past and head for a future that resembles the way other professionals behave. And *that* requires a credible professional body for the field.

What would a professional strategy body do?

Whether progress comes from existing professional institutions, from universities and business schools, or from some combination of both, the minimum aim is clear, and very similar to what can be seen in other professions:

- **A rigorous body of strategy knowledge (BoK).** The BoK should cover all proven and reliable methods in strategy, specifying authoritative sources, and with detailed worked examples. Coverage would also need to include key topics from all other management subjects. It would have to offer both basic and advanced strategy concepts.

- **Graded training.** Whether provided by universities or other training providers, training must be demanding, aligned to the body of knowledge, and take professionals through increasing levels of mastery. It would need to deal with how strategy is applied in a diverse range of sectors, from social networks to natural resources to consumer services, and in a whole range of situations, from entrepreneurial start-up to acquisitions to turn-rounds. Training should also deal with strategy in non-business situations and offer specialties for the public and voluntary sectors.

- **Rigorous certification.** Professional standards are established and enforced by rigorous examinations. The body of knowledge will make clear what those standards are, and a properly moderated examination process will ensure those standards are enforced. As in other professions, a substantial failure rate should be expected, with candidates retaking exams if sufficiently committed.

- **Experience.** No book knowledge will be of much use if it is not applied, so the strategy profession — also like others — must seek evidence of its being competently applied. Merely having spent time in a strategy role will not be enough, either. The requirement will need to be for documentary proof of competent work, endorsed by those for whom the work is done. A common approach is to offer a certification that is essentially provisional to those passing the exams and upgraded to full membership of the profession when the experience requirement is fulfilled.

- **Continuing professional development.** Lastly, respected professions require their members to maintain and build their expertise. This is achieved through additional training and other evidence of active participation in the profession's development, such as conference attendance.

How might young professionals respond to the offer of a qualification standard in strategic management? Would there be an outcry at how reasonable it is to expect professional standards to be set and enforced? If the CFAI experience is anything to go by, quite the opposite is likely. People who invest great effort in learning to perform demanding professional work expect their achievement to be recognized. As the CFA standard has spread, not just in the US but around the world, enrolment in its examinations has shot up rapidly, in spite of — or perhaps because of — an increasing failure rate.

However, there are special features of strategy work that impose a few adjustments on the standard professional model.

First, since strategy work has little respect, it has not until now offered a full-time career for almost anyone except consultants. Strategy jobs are usually held for short periods of time by executives on other career paths, especially those aspiring to general management. At best, it is treated as a useful development role for anyone aspiring to a top position. But this view should be challenged. As one global corporation's Chief Strategy Officer told me "It really annoys me that every head-hunter I hear from brings me strategy jobs with the promise that 'it's just a stepping stone to CEO' as if head of strategy was somehow not a valid senior position in its own right, like CFO or VP of Marketing or HR. I don't expect or want to be CEO of this or any other company. Several colleagues in operations, marketing and finance would be better for the top job. But strategy is what I'm real good at – I know stuff and can do stuff that they wouldn't have a clue about, and what I do makes a massive difference to this company's future."

This disrespect for strategy jobs means that many are occupied by amateurs who have no grounding in the topic. Given that no professional training or testing currently exists in strategy, it is quite unrealistic to expect certification at mid- and senior levels to backfill all the know-how required at the analyst level. But a professional institute *could* establish standards for the minimum that managers and leaders with aspects of strategy to their jobs need to know, and set training and testing requirements accordingly. Not all such executives may be thrilled at the idea of being required to obtain such training in strategy. However, as we have noted, there is a real hunger for strategy understanding amongst managers in all functions, so we might reasonably expect a strong uptake of such an offering, especially from the best.

The broadest view

A second roadblock to establishing a professional model of strategy is that strategy is, almost by definition, not the stovepipe capability that mostly suffices in other functions: a marketing VP need not know much about HR and an IT VP need not know much about R&D. Strategy analysts, managers, and leaders, in contrast *do* need to know at least some essentials of the main functions of other departments to be competent in their jobs. No strategy professional should be ignorant of basic accounting principles, market research and marketing methods, or how IT contributes to an organisation's functioning. The training and testing at each level, then, would have to include such bare essentials from those functions.

Lastly, strategic management is critical in all sectors, not just in industry and commerce, but also in public services, government, and not-for-profit organisations. Clearly, some strategically important issues in corporate cases, such as marketing or product development, are less relevant in some of those cases. Equally, there are issues in those domains that are not relevant in business cases. This implies a need for different flavours of training and testing for different sectors. A related opportunity may exist in the form of specialisations that professionals could pursue, depending on which part of the corporate sector they operate in.

Setting up such training and testing may seem a daunting prospect, but it has been done in other professions—and the institute itself would not have to do it. Universities and other organisations can provide the training itself, given a clear curriculum, and testing, too, can be outsourced.

The essential roles of a professional body in strategy, then, would be to define the required knowledge, facilitate the development of training in that knowledge, and establish the testing program leading to recognised certification. After establishing this foundation, the professional body would then provide useful functions, also to be found in other professions, such as bringing practitioners, advisers (consultants in this case), and academics together to enforce relevance and drive up knowledge and performance across the field.

Having summarised what a professional body in strategy would need to do, the next question is where such a body might come from.

Create a profession out of existing institutions

There appear to be three main options: build an institution from the ground up, extend out from already-established bodies in related areas, or develop from the fledgling strategy associations that already exist.

In principle, it might be possible to establish a professional body from nothing. It might be conceivable, for example, that consulting firms and/ or senior corporate strategy executives such as CSOs could work together to fund, establish, and guide the emergence of a whole new institution. Given the weak state of the profession and the conflicting interests of consultants, however, this seems unlikely, and other options may be simpler and faster in any case.

Maybe a strategy profession can be made a focus of some institute with a wider coverage of management issues. Any candidate would need both the motivation and capability to pursue this opportunity. Let's consider a couple of examples.

The American Management Association (AMA)[5], for example, is a powerful body in the US. It offers training and certificate programmes, which reflect the AMA's focus on establishing real-world methods to address relevant business issues as identified by business leaders. It is also good to see that these programmes offer "practical hands-on and immediately applicable processes...supported by actual case studies and real successes—not untested academic theories."

Unfortunately, although the AMA's program includes some coverage of strategic management, it is very limited, and a respectable professional certification would need more demanding and rigorous training and testing than the AMA appears to offer.

The UK's Chartered Management Institute (CMI)[6] is another dominant body in its country of origin and has the added kudos of official recognition. (In the UK, an organisation can only become a "Chartered Institute" after fulfilling demanding criteria and proving that it is representative of the community it serves, which may not be the case in all jurisdictions). This Institute, like the AMA, is large, influential, and has, if anything, even broader reach into management, with explicit support for a range of public sectors as well as for business management.

The CMI offers an extensive program of training,[7] covering many fields of management, up to the most senior levels. The top two levels of training include references to strategy, but it is not evident that the training covers much of the necessary territory or is based on rigorous foundations, since there is no reference to a body of knowledge on the topic. It is possible, though, that the CMI could broaden its strategy offering, for example, with more specific strategy training and certification for lower levels of management.

Similar management institutes and associations can be found in many countries, many offering training and certification. However, none have a sufficient focus on strategy to contribute to defining and establishing professionalism in the discipline, whether amongst junior executives or senior leaders. Strategy needs its own dedicated organisation, content, processes, and structures, rather than being a subsidiary of a broader institution.

So although it is not inconceivable that a professional strategy body might be grown out of an existing management association, it is not clear that this is any more likely than a green-field initiative—which leaves

154

us with existing associations and institutes with a focus on strategy.

There is an American Strategic Management Institute (ASMI),[8] but neither its focus nor its activities seem to match its title. The ASMI's mission is "to identify, study, and disseminate the leading strategic management and performance measurement practices pioneered by best-in-class organisations." It claims to be the nation's leading authority on measurement and management methodologies for improving individual and organisational performance. Its Corporate Performance Logic Model offers to connect various planning activities—employee plans, sourcing, IT, activity-based costing, a strategic plan, and more—into a single overarching process. However, there is little sign of sound strategy principles behind this model. Its training services focus on administrative management, and it offers a curious assortment of "centres of excellence": performance benchmarking, HR management, knowledge-assistant training, strategic communications and healthcare.

A few bodies focused on strategy do seem to have spotted the need for a solid body of knowledge in the field that supports graded training and certification. The Strategic Management Institute of Australia[9] offers a promising model, aimed at graduate and post-graduate students as well as experienced executives. It takes candidates up three levels of attainment: Affiliate, Associate, and Fellow. The first two levels include formal study, but all levels also require relevant practical experience, plus evidence of continued study. However, the training program consists of just two core courses in strategy, plus a short list of electives—promising, but not sufficient in depth or breadth.

The US-based Association of Strategic Planning[10] also offers professional certification in strategy. There is much information on the philosophy of the Association, the training available, and the design of the certification structure. There is also a large amount of information on the body of knowledge upon which the whole system is built. It is heavily oriented towards interpersonal considerations and the process of getting strategy done. Although it refers to strategy "content", there is little evidence that the training or certification offer any substantive coverage of rigorous, reliable tools or methods. Hardly their fault, you may argue, given the weaknesses of what is available in any case. Unfortunately, it leaves what is offered looking more like the personal preferences of the Association's leaders, rather than an objective and comprehensive coverage of the discipline.

The Canadian Business Strategy Association[11] defines a body of knowledge for strategy, covering both business-unit and corporate level issues, as well as implementation. It offers levels of professional certification (confusingly referred to as "accreditation", a term usually indicating approval of courses and institutions, rather than individuals). Certification does not appear to require any examination, but relies instead on candidates passing approved university courses and evidence of professional experience. Though a promising start, it suffers from the weakness in strategy's methods and teaching, and the base level of certification appears to require only that candidates have achieved a modest pass level in just two strategy-related courses during their degree. It seems unlikely that a professional body in accountancy or law, say, would offer any certification on the basis of covering just two courses in a whole degree program.

Well-meaning and promising though these initiatives are, a serious profession needs more. The best known professions feature the substantial and continuous involvement of practitioners and advisers, as well as academics and training bodies. Top law firms are heavily involved in maintaining the integrity of the legal profession; top accounting firms and CFOs are actively engaged in the accounting profession. On a smaller scale, the International Council on Systems Engineering[12] also brings together universities, consulting firms, and employers of systems engineers to steer the development of the profession, even with a membership of just 5,000 people. The Chartered Financial Analyst Institute (CFAI)[13] appears to be an exception, drawing on relatively little participation from the employers of its members and instead relying largely on the strong backing of universities and training providers. But this achievement is easily explained by the burgeoning growth and massive financial value of the sectors the CFAI serves, together with the fact that its whole industry effectively consists of the knowledge and skills of its professionals.

Where might we look for similarly wide scope and scale in strategy? The Strategic Management Society (SMS)[14] should be able to offer such a lead, since it focuses exclusively on strategy and claims membership from all three of the key stakeholder groups: academics, managers, and consultants. It also has an international membership and reach. But the SMS has only 3,000 members (just 3 percent of the CFAI!) and has been mostly abandoned by the professionals, who have left it largely to the academics. Nevertheless, the Society takes seriously the problems of poor strategy practice, and at the present time is actively seeking to build a body of knowledge, on which certification could be based.

156

The UK-based Society for Professional Strategy (SPS, formerly the Strategic Planning Society)[15] has long had a focus on strategy practitioners. It, too, is small and just now starting to recover from a number of difficult years. Central to this rebirth is a focus on bringing strategy practitioners into touch with universities and teachers. In March 2012, the Society held a small conference to discuss how it might be possible for strategy to step up several gears and make the topic truly professional.

It appears then that, although all are currently small, the SMS, SPS, some other body, or an alliance of such groups could attempt a breakthrough, but they will need others to move, too.

More amateurs please!

Given the appalling damage caused by bad strategic management up to and during the 2008–09 recession, you might imagine that any effort to improve matters would be welcome. But on the same day the SPS held its meeting on making strategy more professional, the Financial Times described the idea as "faintly comical"[16], envisioning a world in which academics idly speculate (which is in fact where we are starting from!) while executives struggle to cope with a future no one can predict. The article neglected to mention, as noted at the beginning of this book, that corporations actually cause most recessions, and that, as we have also noted, successful organisations do not so much "forecast" the future as create it.

Citing anecdotal comments that managers still rank experience as much more important than skill, the article lauds Microsoft's 2005 appointment of an "ambidextrous" CEO from Walmart. Now this particular cross-industry appointment—one of many tens of thousands—may well have been successful, but this mystical belief in some indefinable quality is precisely what led the Royal Bank of Scotland to appoint CEO Fred Goodwin, who led the company's charge to the top of the hill (during which he was awarded a British Knighthood!) and its subsequent tumble to the bottom (after which the award was unceremoniously taken back).

The Financial Times, it seems, would prefer to see more Fred Goodwins leading our major corporations, rather than support even a tentative attempt to do better.

Just consider this. Here we have arguably the most respected, authoritative business newspaper in the world, read by and influencing much of the planet's corporate leadership — a newspaper that, with government ministers, top businesspeople, and other serious journals, has spent the last three years wringing its hands about how the worst recession since the 1930s came about. Yet its response to a serious effort to do something about the current state of affairs is a trivial and ill-informed dismissal of the whole idea of strategy, with not a single serious comment on the need, practical issues, or potential benefits of making strategy professional.

The others: universities and consultants

Universities awake from their slumber

Some universities appear to have seen an opportunity in the absence of focused strategy education: we are starting to see the emergence of Masters' qualifications in Strategy (see for example, courses offered by France's Hautes Etudes Commerciales de Paris (HEC)[17], the Netherlands' Tilburg University[18], and the Vienna University of Economics and Business[19]; curiously, the opportunity seems to have been picked up more strongly in Europe than elsewhere). If these programs could just be bound strongly to practical exposure to real strategy challenges in substantial organisations, they could provide some of the professional foundations required.

The courses come in a variety of flavours but generally offer a wide-ranging and substantive set of courses covering most of the important topics in strategy. Many of the universities offering these Masters' programs are accredited by the respected inspecting bodies mentioned at the end of Chapter 5: the Advanced Association of Collegiate Schools of Business (AACSB)[20] and the European Foundation for Management Development's Quality Improvement System (EQUIS)[21].

Time for the consultants to step up

The elephants in the room in all of this — or not in the room as yet — are the powerful, global strategy consulting firms, who have been strangely absent from the discussion of what needs to be done.

These firms probably contain the greatest concentration of real strategy skill that exists and could be of real help in raising standards elsewhere. They could, for example, go beyond the brief articles they put out in their house journals and publish detailed, rigorous reference material on how strategy should be developed and implemented. A great example of what could be done exists in the outstanding finance book Valuation from the experts at McKinsey & Company.[22]

The consulting firms could also contribute greatly to the strategy education of emerging managers. They possess exactly the kind of detailed, factual information on real-world challenges that is totally lacking in the case studies taught in business schools. Concern with client confidentiality can easily be managed: when pitching for strategy projects with potential clients, they are already only too happy to share disguised information on similar cases.

McKinsey, BCG, Monitor, and the others could also support and contribute to the efforts to establish professional standards and certification. They probably stand to benefit rather little from such a development (they get on just fine with their own skill-building), but it is to be hoped that they might take a rather more responsible stance and contribute positively. They know better than most what methods and skills are needed, and have vast resources, not just money, but also knowledge and experience, to bring to the effort. It might be hoped that at least a handful of recently retired partners would feel the aim is worth supporting and commit to doing so.

Strategy skill for all

Neither a Masters-level education in strategy nor the certification efforts of emerging professional associations will hit the immediate and critical target: the current and mid-term future practice of strategy by senior leaders who never have taken, and likely never will take, the trouble to get trained. But we might at least hope those leaders will get to "know what they don't know" and seek to hire and deploy people with demonstrable capability to help them.

This is already common in other areas, of course. CEOs who do not happen to be finance experts are expected to turn to people who are, to ensure the financial well-being of their organisations. Business leaders in sectors with substantial operational or financial risk are expected to

159

turn to risk experts to avoid exposing their organisations to danger. Such expectations cannot prevent mismanagement or dishonest treatment of finance or risk, but at least when it happens we know whom to hold to account—either the advisers who messed up or the leadership who ignored sound advice.

We have already noted that most strategic management is done by people with other responsibilities and is not, as yet, a self-contained career path for anyone but consultants. But we have also pointed out that a rigorous body of knowledge can also be used to specify skill requirements for people in those temporary strategy roles and to design focused, short-course training in the minimum skills they require.

And there are, in any case, signs that this view of strategy as a temporary role for gifted amateurs is changing. The role of Chief Strategy Officer was almost unheard of a decade ago, but a 2008 study by Accenture found it was an increasingly common job title in major corporations.[23] Furthermore, these jobs are being filled by people with solid credentials for doing strategy (albeit lacking formal qualification or professional status), and CEOs, CFOs, and others look to the incumbents for advice on critical issues that are not on anyone else's radar. In particular, Accenture note, CSOs keep guard over what they call "horizon two", the critical period of one to four years out, between current-year performance and long-term vision. If only all corporations had had such a focus leading up to 2008!

In conclusion

This brief discussion of how a strategy profession might emerge has done no more than scratch the surface. Many highly experienced executives, consultants, and academics have the expertise and stature to clarify what must be done and the influence to make it happen. There must surely be some people in the field with the ability and will to challenge the status quo. What we need them to do is drive a hard-nosed initiative to develop and establish the kinds of institutions, structures, and disciplines we find in other professions.

Perhaps some of the outstanding strategy consultants who have made their pile of cash will see the value of committing their authority and influence to such an effort. Perhaps a few of the seasoned top executives who have struggled to cope with feeble strategy tools and dismal advice during their careers will see the value in helping establish a more solid and reliable foundation upon which to base the work of strategy. Perhaps those rare academics who understand the possible application of their science in the real world will stop wringing their hands about why no one uses their work and see some value in helping to find what is useful and get it used rigorously and professionally. We can only hope that change will be driven from within the existing community of strategy practitioners.

Notes

The majority of notes for this chapter are weblinks - for ease of access they are also listed on the books' website - www.troublewithstrategy.com

1. https://www.cfainstitute.org/
2. http://www.cfainstitute.org/cfaprogram/Documents/cfa_charter_brochure.pdf
3. http://www.cfainstitute.org/cfaprogram/courseofstudy/Pages/index.aspx
4. For information on this and other regulations, see www.sec.gov/rules/ http://www.amanet.org/
5. http://www.amanet.org/
6. http://www.managers.org.uk/
7. http://www.managers.org.uk/management-qualifications
8. http://www.asmiweb.com/
9. http://www.smiknowledge.com/certified-strategy-practitioner.html
10. http://www.strategyplus.org/
11. http://www.thecbsa.org/
12. http://www.incose.org/
13. https://www.cfainstitute.org/pages/index.aspx
14. http://www.smsweb.org/
15. http://sps.org.uk/
16. http://www.ft.com/cms/s/0/b95ef8ce-6c2b-11e1-b00f-00144feab49a.html#axzz1p1lUSpQa
17. http://www.hec.edu/MSc/Programs/Masters-in-Strategic-Management-MS-MSc
18. http://www.tilburguniversity.edu/education/masters-programmes/strategic-management/
19. http://www.wu.ac.at/programs/en/master/simc
20. http://www.aacsb.edu/accreditation/
21. http://www.efmd.org/index.php/accreditation-main/equis
22. Tim Koller, Marc Goedhart, and David Wessels, 2010, Valuation: Measuring and Managing the Value of Companies, Fifth Edition, Hoboken, NJ: John Wiley & Sons, Inc.
23. Tim Breene, Paul F. Nunes, and Walt Shill, 2008, Rise of the Chief Strategy Officer, Accenture. Retrieved 4-2-2012.

APPENDIX 1

A CONTRIBUTION TO METHOD

It is not the purpose of this book to promote my own ideas.[1] On the other hand, if I do not mention it at all, I may be accused of bringing only problems, not solutions. No single contribution can solve all the problems of weak theory, method, and tools in strategy, but what follows would seem to have at least a little to offer, though it is up to others to judge. So here goes: the approach is best termed "strategy dynamics". The method is essentially simple, but as we have discussed, theory does not have to be complicated to be useful.

1. Focus on performance over time

The method starts by addressing the correct question: how *absolute* performance can grow, sustainably, over time. In corporate cases with an orientation to delivering value to investors, **management want a cash flow forecast!**

Where other kinds of objective are pursued, whether in the public or voluntary sectors, or in businesses for which investor value creation is not the primary motivation, the correct question still comes in the same form: focusing on change over time. Whether the aim is raising levels of education or health, reducing crime rates, or alleviating suffering, strategy is about how performance on those indicators can be improved and sustained over time. The explanation that follows is oriented to business value but can be generalised for any other purpose.

163

Three standard questions need to be answered (see Figure 8):

- **Why** has performance followed its particular path up to the present time? This question is important because the answer will contain important information on how the enterprise actually works in relation to the environment in which it operates.

- Where is that performance likely to go into the future under (a) business-as-usual conditions, or (b) less benign conditions? This establishes the baseline of performance for the improvement that a strategy might achieve.

- How can management improve that future performance trajectory? This answer must encompass every decision and action that could significantly alter that trajectory, across all functions of the business, recognising the interdependence between them, and must be continually updated.

For research into business strategy, this implies replacing the question "Why does firm A deliver higher return on invested capital than firm B?" with "Why does firm A deliver stronger, sustained growth in free cash flow than firm B?" It is from free cash flow, after all, that investors are paid!

Figure 8: Improving performance over time

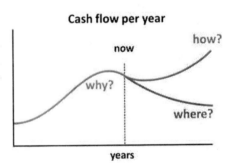

2. Current performance depends directly on the current quantity of resources

The answer to the question in step 1 is most easily demonstrated by following the logic of a financially oriented business case. If we want to know what drives *growth* in cash flow, we first need to explain *current* cash flow. Luckily, this is dead easy, because the accountants have given us an unequivocal answer, at least enough to get started. Current profit and cash flow is clearly and simply explained by the income and cash flow statements:

- Profit is revenue minus costs.

- Revenue is sales multiplied by price.

Drilling further back to find what drives sales and costs:

- Sales come from customers. If everything else is equal, including customer size, then twice as many customers equals twice the sales rate. (This is where we part company with the finance approach that views sales as coming from market size and share — these are results, not causes).

- Costs are driven by the resources deployed to win, support, and serve those customers: mostly staff and capacity. Again, holding everything else constant, twice as many staff equals twice as much staff cost, and twice as much capacity equals twice as much operating cost. (Another departure from the finance view, this time from the idea that costs are driven by percentages of revenue).

This is not quite the full story on costs, however:

- Certain management decisions immediately affect profits. A 10-percent higher price, if nothing changes, gives 10 percent more revenue, and doubling our marketing or training efforts doubles the costs of those items.

- Current performance also reflects certain external conditions. If customers generally are spending 20 percent less, then our revenue will be 20 percent lower.

- Costs also arise from *acquiring* or *developing* resources, not just from having them: hiring staff, building capacity, and developing the products or services we offer.

165

Of course, everything else is not equal: customers vary in value, staff vary in how much they cost us, and capacity costs may change with scale and experience.

The implications for research into strategy and performance are simple. Any explanation for profit or cash flow cannot leap over the basic financials of how a business makes money, but must explain the revenue and costs from which profit and cash flow derive.

3. The first critical piece! Resources accumulate over time.

This is the single, massively important mechanism that correlation-based explanations for business performance and recommendations for strategy fail to deal with. The principle is deadly simply, but fundamental, not just to business but to how the world works in general.

To understand this mechanism, consider what "explains" the amount of money in your personal bank account. That sum *may* be correlated with how much money you earn, how many kids you have, where you live, your personal lifestyle, and scores of other possible explanations. (Remember the 18 factors that PIMS claims explain performance from Chapter 3?). But a wealthy person could have a hugely negative bank balance, and a person with a lower income could have a very large one. The only accurate explanation is simple:

> **The cash in your bank account today is precisely the sum of every dollar that was ever paid in, minus every dollar that was ever paid out.**

This is not an opinion, a theory, or a statistical observation: it is a simple, self-evident, and irrefutable truth or "axiom" about how the world works. It has an equally simple and irrefutable consequence.

> **The cash in your bank account today is precisely the amount that was in there yesterday (or at any other point in the past),**

166

plus what has been added, minus what has been taken out, since that time.

The same is true, of course, for corporate cash, but it is also true of anything else that accumulates over time, including customers, staff, capacity, product range, and other items:

- The number of customers you have today is the number you had last year, plus any won, minus any lost over that time.

- The number of staff employed today is the number employed last month, plus any hired, minus any lost or fired.

- The amount of capacity you have today is the amount you had ten years ago, plus any you added, minus any you closed.

- The number of products you offer is the number you offered three years ago, plus any new products you launched during that time, minus any you discontinued.

There can be no other explanation!

All items that exhibit this behaviour are technically termed "asset stocks" (because they are stocks of assets!) or simply stocks. In this approach to strategy, they are what we define as "resources". "Strategic" resources are simply those that have a significant impact on how performance changes over time. Not all do: inventory, orders, and debtors, for example, are usually insignificant, but in the rare cases where they are significant, such as in the case of Boeing's order book or Exxon's inventory of oil reserves, these too become strategic.

*In terms of our quest to explain performance, the mechanism has vitally important implications. If no other factor can explain the current quantity of resources in the business, except its own history of gains and losses, then neither can any such factor explain anything that **depends** on those resources, including revenue, costs, profits, and cash flow. If your theory does not include the mathematics of all significant accumulating asset stocks, then it cannot be valid.*

167

4. The second critical piece! The rate of resource growth at any time depends on existing resources already in place.

We have established that (1) we are trying to explain how performance changes; (2) performance at each point in time depends on resources; and (3) those resources accumulate and deplete over time. The next, and final, step therefore is to identify what causes those rates of change in resource growth.

Some rates of change are dead easy to determine because we just make a decision. We want to add capacity, so we just build it. We want more delivery vehicles, so we just buy or rent them. Some are not quite so easy to determine, however. We want more staff, so we set about hiring them, but the new hires may not be so easy to find and may need training to be effective once in place. Some may be easy enough to decide upon but take time to accomplish—developing new products, for example.

Some resources, though, are really tough to acquire and to hold on to. The obvious example is customers. If only we could just flick a switch and add 50 percent to our customer base or prevent all future customer losses!

These and other rates of change are known as resource "flow rates" because they describe the rate (units per time period) at which resources are "flowing" into or out of the system.

Resource flow rates control strategic performance.

Since current performance depends on current resources, then any change in performance can only arise (other conditions being constant) from resources being won or lost. It is therefore at the flow rates—and only at the flow rates—that management control the trajectory of future performance. And their ability to control some critical resource flow rates is heavily dependent on existing resources. For example:

- The customer win rate depends on numbers of salespeople, and/ or product range, and/or points of presence (such as retail stores, another resource).

- The customer loss rate depends on the adequacy of customer service, and hence on the number of service staff or else on the adequacy of capacity to supply them.

- The rate of new product development depends on the number of skilled developers.

- The rate of staff losses depends on work pressure, reflecting the workload driven by customers.

Two special dependencies also arise:

- A resource's growth or decline will often reflect its own current quantity. Customers may recommend others to buy from you, for example, or may leave you if you cannot adequately serve the customers you already have.

- Resource growth or decline may also reflect the quantity of potential resource available. Hiring people when there are none available will be tough, as will winning customers in a saturated market.

A final point to note about these relationships between resources and their flow rates: *this* is where the uncertainty about strategy and performance is concentrated. The relationships among resources, revenues, costs, profits, and cash flows are simple and clearly defined. The mathematics of how resources accumulate and deplete over time is, as explained, even more deterministic.

The only place left, then, where there can be any uncertainty is what causes resources to be won and lost at the rate they are. Why are customers not being won twice as fast, or lost half as quickly? Why are we losing key staff twice as fast as competitors? Why does it take us half the time to develop new products?

For any theory of strategy to explain how performance changes over time, it **must** *explain how resources, too, change over time.*

169

The "Strategic Architecture" of a Business.

Combining steps 1 to 4 above results in an objective, integrated, and coherent model of how a business or other organisation actually functions and performs. It also has some vital characteristics:

- All the language can be clearly defined and agreed upon.

- All relationships in the system are explicit and can be tested and proven.

- Constructing such a diagnosis is repeatable: two adequately trained professionals would go through the same process, seeking the same information, processing it in the same way, and arriving at the same result.

This much is only a minimal starting point but can easily be extended to make it more comprehensive. But even this basic core can explain much of how an organisation performs over time. In many cases, even answering the question of why customers are won and lost at the rate they are can be enough to transform growth in sales and profits. (Amazingly many companies do not even know what these two numbers are!) In other cases, solving the imbalance among customers, demand, and capacity can be enough to release a firm's growth potential.

However, for more complex challenges and for a richer understanding, important extensions must be added.

Resource quality. Customers are not all equal, and they contribute differentially to sales and profits. Staff also vary in their contributions to output and quality. Products appeal to different numbers and types of customer. Such qualities of a resource can be quantified as "attributes" of the resource to which they belong. They are won when a unit of resource is won, they are lost when the resource itself is lost, and can be changed whilst the resource remains with us.

Resource development. Resources often develop through stages, during each of which their contribution to the progress of the whole system changes.

170

Customers may be aware of us but not buy from us or may be loyal or disloyal. Staff grow through stages of experience and seniority. Products drive different cost rates at each stage of development and once launched may contribute differently as the move from being novel to being established or obsolete. Capacity and other assets may deteriorate through characteristic stages, being reliable and high-performing at first, then falling in performance and reliability as they age.

Competitive rivalry. Neither the core resource system nor these additional mechanisms are usually immune from competition. Indeed, the essence of competition is most often about winning and retaining customers, so the dynamics of customer development, gain, and loss must be captured, quantified, and explained.

Add to these mechanisms the common need to break down the challenge by different segments (customer type, size, or region), to deal with different categories of staff, and to recognise different product groups, and it will become apparent how an essentially simple set of core principles can readily become quite complex.

However, the resulting "theory" is still robust, fulfilling standard requirements:

- **It is general:** It applies to all organisations, in all situations, at all times. It is also applicable at all levels, being just as valid for issues in small parts of a business or specific departments as it is for an entire business or a multi-business corporation.

- **It is useful:** Knowing how the system works, and where and how in that system decisions made by management change the trajectory of performance, by how much, over what period of time, at what cost, is likely to be helpful.

- **It is true:** The logic of the argument and causal relationships the theory captures are completely explicit, quantifiable, and open to the scientific acid test: can it be falsified? I am no theoretician, but I can see no way in which the relationships described here could be shown to be untrue (but that's for others to challenge).

171

The theory can also be extended. The old static frameworks of the "positioning" school of strategy can be made more useful by incorporating them into a dynamic model of strategy. Entry and exit of firms to and from an industry is evidently a time-based phenomenon, so simply showing that the threat of such changes may affect profitability is of limited value. It is much more helpful to show how firms of certain sizes enter, grow, or leave an industry at varying rates, and the likely implications for the ability of your firm to grow its own revenue and cash flow.

Those who believe abstract, intangible factors are critical can add these to the model. Yes, of course, reputation, staff motivation, investor confidence, and similar soft issues matter. But *if* they matter, then they *must* exert their influence through the structure of the relationships outlined above. There is no way for reputation to affect revenue and cash flow, for example, except through the gains, losses, and purchase rate of customers. This and other intangibles can be specified, quantified, added to the core of the system, and their impact on how performance changes over time can be assessed. Capabilities, the other favourite of the resource based view, can be treated likewise, along with the dynamics of learning and adaptation of strategy.

The model can be extended to the corporate strategy questions of the multi-market, multi-business corporation. The relatedness of business operations that share resources and capabilities is readily made explicit and measurable, as are the dynamics of events and initiatives such as acquisitions and alliances.

> For a full explanation of the method, see Kim Warren, 2008, Strategic Management Dynamics, West Sussex, UK: John Wiley & Sons, Ltd. A shorter description can be found in Kim Warren, 2011, Strategy Dynamics Essentials (eBook), Strategy Dynamics Ltd, also available for Kindle.

> Extensive learning materials can be found on the Strategy Dynamics site: www.strategydynamics.com. Software for mapping and modelling business performance with the strategy dynamics method is available at www.sysdea.com.

172

Notes

1. The theory is not mine in any case, but goes back to seminal work in the 1960s by Professor J. W. Forrester of MIT. It is nothing short of criminal that this powerful and useful explanation for how business (and other fields) actually work and can be managed has remained rejected and ignored for so long. See Jay W. Forrester, 1961, Industrial Dynamics, Waltham, MA: Pegasus Communications.

APPENDIX 2

PROBLEMS WITH CORRELATION

Chapter 3 explained that correlation is a poor method for confirming that a certain cause or causes are driving an organisation's performance. The reason for this is that the math of accumulation—step 3 in the method outlined in Appendix 1—prevents any possibility of a linear relationship between cause and effect in any situation where an accumulating resource sits between the two.

To illustrate this problem and how it arises, consider a simple manufacturing company that wants to understand whether it should spend more or less money on marketing. Management looks at the company's recent history (Figure 9) and sees the patterns for marketing and operating profit shown below.

The charts reflect the following history:

Figure 9: Marketing spend and operating profit history for a company

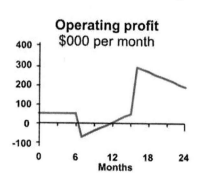

- The company was originally dissatisfied with its low and stagnant profits up to month 6.

- A new head of marketing arrived, who persuaded the company to increase its marketing spend from month 7. This increase in expenditure immediately led to lower profits, as the increase in sales was insufficient to cover the extra cost, although profits started to recover over the following nine months.

- In month 15, the head of finance lost patience with the situation, pointing out that the company had seen a total loss of profits over those nine months of more than $500,000, compared with what they could have expected from just pursuing the original low rate of marketing. He even doubted that the previous rate of marketing was necessary.

- The CEO agreed, so the company cut its marketing spend sharply from month 16. Sure enough, profits jumped as the savings in marketing spend were far greater than the value of lost sales. The head of finance was clearly correct and pointed out to his colleagues that he had made the company over $1.5 million of additional profit over the twelve months since his recommendation, compared with the original low profit rate.

The head of marketing was feeling somewhat dejected about this. Convinced that she was right to increase marketing spend, she commissioned some industry research. The company was one of fifty near-identical firms, and luckily, information on monthly marketing spend and profits was available for all of its competitors.

The next figure shows two results from comparing operating profit with marketing spend for this large sample of companies.

The left-hand graph shows how operating profits in any month compare with marketing spend in that month. The head of marketing was not at all happy with this finding, which suggested that profits were negatively correlated with marketing spend. On reflection, she was not too surprised, since marketing would surely take some time to have its effect, and its immediate impact would of course be an increase in cost.

Perhaps operating profits would increase some months after is the

increase in marketing spend? The head of marketing then looked at how competitors' marketing spend compared with operating profits three months later (right-hand chart, above). Disappointingly, there still seemed to be no positive correlation between marketing spend and profits—but at least the negative relationship had disappeared.

In spite of these apparently approximate and perplexing relationships between marketing spend and profit, the business model at work here is totally deterministic, with no uncertainty whatsoever:

operating profit = revenue − production costs − marketing spend − overhead

sales revenue = customers * sales per customer * unit price

production cost = sales in units * variable cost per unit + fixed production cost

customers today = customers last month + customers won − customers lost

sales per customer = base sales per customer + marketing spend * sales increase per marketing dollar

customers lost = five per month

customers won per month = marketing spend * customers won per marketing dollar

Moreover, the cost of acquiring a customer is $50,000. On average, each customer stays for 20 months before being lost to competitors. During that time, the customer generates 2,000 units of sales per month, on which the gross profit is $40, making a total profit contribution of $80,000. There is no ambiguity whatsoever that every marketing dollar generates $1.60 of value in less than two years.

The figure opposite portrays these relationships diagrammatically.

If the business structure is very simple, why could the head of marketing not discover any correlation between marketing spend and profits? The problem lies at the flow-to-stock boundary. There is no obvious relationship between the number of customers in any month and the win rate of customers in that same month—nor should we be particularly surprised at the lack of such a relationship, since today's number of customers reflects the entire history of customer gains and losses.

This has profound implications for any effort to explain performance outcomes:

- **It is unsafe to seek correlation between any possible causal factor and performance outcomes if any accumulating stock exists between the cause and the outcome.**

- **It is meaningless to seek correlation between asset stocks and the flow rates that determine them—their relationship is precisely defined by the math of integration.**
  Now consider that a real business consists of many accumulating resources, that those resources move through multiple stages, and that the rate at which any is changing reflects other resource quantities, which themselves are subject to the same difficulty. No wonder correlation analysis rarely discovers anything useful about strategy.

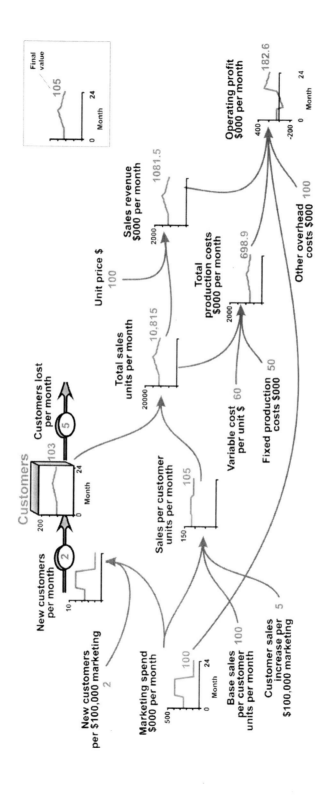

CPSIA information can be obtained
at www.ICGtesting.com
Printed in the USA
FFOW04n1014071215
19358FF

9 781481 120593